FUTURE
TENSE
of
JOY

FUTURE TENSE

JOY

• *a memoir* •

JESSICA TEICH

SEAL PRESS

ISBN 978-1-58005-569-7

Library of Congress Cataloging-in-Publication Data

Names: Teich, Jessica, author.
Title: The future tense of joy : a memoir / Jessica Teich.
Description: Berkeley, California : Seal Press, [2016]
Identifiers: LCCN 2016009576 I ISBN 9781580055697 (hardback)
Subjects: LCSH: Teich, Jessica. I Suicide victims. I Suicide--Social aspects.
  I Women--Psychology. I Authors, American--21st century--Biography. I
  BISAC: BIOGRAPHY & AUTOBIOGRAPHY / Personal Memoirs. I PSYCHOLOGY /
  Suicide. I PSYCHOLOGY / Mental Health.
Classification: LCC HV6545 .T423 2016 I DDC 362.28092--dc23
LC record available at https://lccn.loc.gov/2016009576

Published by
Seal Press
An Imprint of Perseus Books
A Hachette Book Group company
1700 Fourth Street
Berkeley, California
Sealpress.com

Cover design by Laura Klynstra
Interior design by Tabitha Lahr

Printed in the United States of America

9 8 7 6 5 4 3 2 1

For Isabel and Charlotte

AUTHOR'S NOTE

This book is a memoir, but also a mystery—the search for a woman who haunted me, although we never met. Some names have been changed, but all the events are true, described with as much fidelity as possible, based on my own recollection, and on lengthy interviews with the people she loved.

This young woman had a special radiance, an incandescence. She took her own life, which left her friends grasping to understand her power over them. I, too, fell under her spell, and soon she not only bewitched me, she besieged my narrative.

In the end, this book is as much her story as mine.

The memory is a living thing—it too is in transit. But during its moment, all that is remembered joins, and lives—the old and the young, the past and the present, the living and the dead.

—Eudora Welty

INTRODUCTION

Survivors remember the past in pieces. Not necessarily "before" and "after," which would be easier. It's more like time melts into Dali-like puddles, or convulses, slamming together faces and events. Psychologists often speak of a distortion in time afterward, as though the trauma occurred only moments before, but sometimes the pain is so buried it ceases to exist. Then it springs up suddenly, like an allergy, even when it seems there's no irritant. Or descends, like a fine but malevolent mesh.

That was true for me, but I could never write about my experience as a "survivor." Even the word seemed bloodless, badly lit. I'd had so many privileges: an education at Yale, then at Oxford as a Rhodes scholar. I had a lovely husband and children; two daughters with their father's long lashes and love of puns. But I felt trapped behind a scrim, like the smoked glass of an antique mirror, with life on the other side, tantalizing and remote. What happened when *I* was a child was holding me hostage, as surely as if I'd been stolen away.

There is a moment, stepping onto a plane, when you may hesitate at the threshold, nervous to leave the safety of one world, uncertain of the world beyond. This book takes place at that juncture, a crucial moment for my family, when I tried to make the pieces of my life cohere. Its sections are like those shards of experience, but the path they chart is not specific to me. For we have all been broken or betrayed.

Life is the part that happens *after*. When we move toward hope, toward peace, toward the healing of our hearts.

PART ONE

BEGINNINGS

The fear of life . . . is the beginning of all evil.
—Rebecca West

1.

Eight and a half minutes. That's how long it takes to walk from the bus stop to the dance studio, if you're twelve years old and long legged, like my older daughter, Isabel. Especially if you're focused, as I've warned her—repeatedly—to be.

The bus stop, at the corner of Olympic and Stewart, anchors an area in transition. For every sushi bar, there's a gentlemen's club with a name like "Silver Reign" (you can imagine the age of the clientele). There are auto-body shops and acu-therapy clinics and a veterinary hospital advertising its DEDICATED CARING PARTNERS. When I drove past the day before, casing the joint, I thought the sign said DEDICATED CARING *PARENTS*. That's what I'm trying to be.

At the little tabernacle next door, a neon sign beseeches NEED FAITH? Yes, I'm afraid I do.

I need *a lot* of faith because Isabel is a thinker, often lost in a book. She finds the real world less compelling than Narnia or Middle-earth. I've often urged her to live more deeply in three dimensions. So how could I refuse when she wanted to take the school bus to the stop near the dance studio, then walk to class? It was just a little walk: eight and a half minutes.

But I was as shocked as if she'd decided to project herself

astrally to Mars. I wanted to say no, but Michael, my husband, wouldn't let me. "Don't make her feel afraid."

He'd seen her do things—like trying to open a door with her elbows—that he knew my fears had inspired.

"Do you know how many dozens of germs are on door-knobs?" I would ask him.

"It doesn't matter," he'd reply. "There'd be no one left on the planet if you could die from a doorknob or a water fountain or a computer screen."

I hadn't even considered the dangers of water fountains. But I said yes to her anyway. *Of course* she could get off the school bus alone, then proceed to the dance studio.

I was plotting: If she reached the bus stop at 3:46 PM, she would be safely at the dance studio by 3:54 PM.

By 3:30 PM I was in position. I'd parked all the way down Stewart, near the construction site of the new Santa Monica College campus, far enough away that Isabel wouldn't recognize the car. She wouldn't have recognized it anyway, I knew. She wouldn't have been looking.

But she *had* to be looking. For eight and a half minutes, she was the solar center of the universe. She had to pay attention to the scruffy young man pacing back and forth, holding an envelope. What was in the envelope? A kilo of heroin? A knife? And the couple, arguing twenty feet farther down the sidewalk. What if their fight escalated to blows, with my daughter walking past?

Isabel had to be watching out for all this, and more. Wouldn't she? No matter. *I* would be watching. I would follow, several steps behind, until she swung open the door of the Westside School of Ballet.

When Isabel was younger, Michael took dozens of photographs of her in front of those bright yellow caution signs: WARNING: FERAL PIG in Hawaii when she was a baby; DANGEROUS SURF near a beach in Laguna when she was six; FALLING ICE next to the ski lift in Mammoth when she was seven; BEWARE ELECTRICAL SHOCK at an artist's studio when she was nine. He did it for me, because he wanted me to believe the world was safe.

Needless to say, I was unconvinced.

I feared that she might sense my presence. We were connected that way. I, too, was remote, a reader, a dancer.

So, of course, I hid. Midway between the bus stop and the ballet school. The shrubbery was hardly concealing: mostly sad-looking ivy and impatiens embarrassed to be taking up space. I managed to find a small bend in the bushes, strewn with discarded sandwiches and cigarette butts and a used condom. Yuck.

Quickly, I found a place that offered better camouflage. I was on a mission. I would not be daunted by a busted beer bottle and a packet of Cheetos coated with dirt.

A flash of bright yellow: the school bus approaching.

I knelt behind the shrub.

3:46 PM, like clockwork, Isabel disembarked, the skirt of her school uniform hiked up dangerously. Dangerously, because she could earn a demerit slip if it was more than "a cellphone and a half" above her knee. (When did the cellphone become a unit of measurement?) Her shirttail ventured out from beneath her cardigan, and she was wearing both shoes, which was a good sign. Last year she got off the school bus wearing only one shoe. How do you lose *one* shoe during the school day?

As she approached, I hunched down farther. Something crunched beneath my boot. I didn't dare think what it might be. Years ago, I proudly took our new puppy for a walk, parading her like a prom queen, only to glance back and see her devouring half of a dead raccoon. I hoped the other half wasn't underneath my feet.

* * *

The corner of Stewart and Olympic featured a cacaphony of white and yellow lines, and three plastic posts jutting out of the pavement, like Popsicle sticks. Next to the sticks was a curved area painted with stripes; then a single lane; then a double yellow lane with insouciant white dashes; then an opposing lane, and a stop sign smack in the middle. Isabel had to negotiate all that just to get from one side of the street to the other. She might as well have been surfing the Farallon straits.

This intersection was livelier than Times Square: a scrum of boys with skateboards; a day laborer in a Dodgers cap; a huddle of scruffy Silicon Valley–types, looking more distracted than dangerous. They could be counted on to destroy our children's minds, but probably not to menace them.

There was a motorcyclist who didn't slow down, let alone stop, at the stop sign. STOP means "soft tap on pedal"—I learned that at traffic school—but he didn't even do that. A man wearing docksiders leaned against a telephone pole. Had a guy in boat shoes ever terrorized anyone? Another man sported a t-shirt that read "Nobody knows I'm gay."

A boy raced by on his bicycle, holding his phone instead of the handlebars. He wasn't wearing a helmet. I wondered if his mother knew. A little girl clattered past in her tap shoes. This corner felt almost exhilarating, like a microcosm of the world.

Years ago, in a children's bookstore, I heard the mother of a toddler ask, "Do you have a DVD he can watch of someone going to the grocery store and the post office and the bank?"

Just take *him to the grocery store and the post office and the bank,* I wanted to tell her. *Let him live in the real world. He'll love it. And as long as he's strapped in his stroller, he'll be safe.*

Isabel stopped at the crosswalk, looked left, then left again. When she reached the middle, near the stop sign, she looked right, then right again. All of which was fine, except that, each time she looked, she also gestured with undulating arms, her mermaid hair flowing behind her. She looked more like a synchronized swimmer than a pedestrian. There's a difference between really looking and *performing* the act of looking. I'd have to talk with her about that when she got home.

But the only trouble she encountered was at the door of the studio. She was shouldering her dance bag, satin ribbons trailing, and a backpack no self-respecting Sherpa would lift. She had to turn *sideways* to fit through the doorway.

Another point for discussion.

But when I went to pick her up that first day, all I said was, "How was class?"

"Good."

"How was taking the bus to class?"

"Good."

But I knew better. I knew that she had traversed the Bermuda Triangle and barely survived.

Every day for the next week, between 3:32 PM and 3:55 PM, I hid in the bushes. I found a deerstalker in my closet, a relic of my graduate student days, and thought it made the perfect disguise. In Southern California, you rarely need a tweed hat, especially one with earflaps and a pair of built-in visors. But the cap had finally come in handy, although I resembled Sherlock Holmes less than Inspector Clouseau.

Day after day, I saw many of the same men, loitering. They would nod to me as I lowered myself into the bushes, awaiting Isabel's bus. I recognized the dog groomer who regularly parked here to smoke weed. The guy with bulging biceps, haranguing his parking meter. The pizza delivery man.

Another baby ballerina hurried past. *Just you wait!* I wanted to warn her mother. *It gets harder; they get bigger; they want more. Soon your tiny person will demand her freedom.*

Soon you'll be waiting here, just like me.

Every afternoon at approximately 3:46 PM, Isabel got off the bus, gesturing to the right and to the left, never really looking at the cars themselves, or making eye contact with the drivers, or any of the other things I had taught her to do. Sometimes she added a little pirouette. I would have to talk to her about that, too.

But how could I? She didn't even know I was there. I came to wonder whether pre-teens, like infants, have a sense of object impermanence. When I wasn't with her, I ceased to exist.

But she and her younger sister were the strongest reasons for my existence. To nurture them and help them thrive. To let them feel their freedom, that endless, elastic feeling when the time between school and supper feels completely unbounded. I remembered lying in the grass as a little girl, ear to the ground, listening for the other side of the world. Life seemed mysterious, but also intelligible, reliable. There were rules, but it didn't matter if you didn't know them. You would discover them soon enough. Was that still true, even now?

When would I—could I—hand my older daughter over to the universe? How would I ever feel that she was safe?

After a week, when my vigil at the corner of Stewart and Olympic began to resemble a sit-in, I could tell by the lemony light that a heat wave was coming on. I'd have to trade my deerstalker for a straw hat. Luckily, I had a closetful. But would that make me more conspicuous?

As I mulled this over from my perch in the bushes, Isabel approached, and I pulled my cap deeper over my ears.

Then she said, evenly, "Mommy, I can see you. I know you're watching."

She kept walking, calling back over her shoulder, "Besides, it's a crosswalk, not a crack den."

I sprang up, brushing aside the leaves and the litter of wrappers, not to greet her, or to make light of the absurdity of my situ-ation, but to demand: "HOW DO YOU EVEN KNOW WHAT A CRACK DEN IS?"

In that moment, I recognized my madness. My fears had made me crazy enough to stalk my own daughter. (Which, admittedly, is better than stalking someone else's daughter.) I couldn't do this anymore.

I had to let Isabel go, so she could *feel* her life, all the luck of it, the beauty and sweetness and surprise.

She was ready to be free.

She was as equipped for freedom as any twelve-year-old could be.

She was *longing* to be free.

And so was I.

But I was dogged by more than a fear of dirty doorknobs. What frightened me was harder to quantify, or disinfect. I was afraid of proximity to other people, all of whom seemed inscruta-ble, volatile. I routinely left an empty stool on either side of me at a sushi bar, or fled the elevator if another passenger seemed unwell. I never accepted a tissue from someone's pocket, or a Tic Tac from her purse. But it was one thing for me to live in the thrall of all these fugitive fears. Now I was dragging Isabel—and soon, her little sister, Charlotte—into captivity.

That's when I knew I had to change, to confront my fear of pit bulls and gas meters and cold sores. Michael had been waiting for me, *wanting* me to change, but I never could. Then I saw my daughter struggling under the weight of a burden heavier than any backpack.

My children were my reason for being.

They would be my reason to begin.

2.

That night, I was lying awake, thinking about Isabel, thinking about that crosswalk, thinking about Charlotte, who had just turned six. Outside the bedroom window, the owls hooted furiously, or maybe that was Michael snoring. What's more, he was a snoring *denier,* which even in a loved one can be maddening.

Down the hall, our daughters slept, warm and flushed and hopeful, the sound of their breathing usually a comfort, but not tonight. So I wandered downstairs to the living room, seeking solace in the stillness of objects: the tilt of the lampshades, the stoicism of the couch.

On the coffee table was a pile of magazines, perpetually unread, and I grabbed one, expecting it to be a copy of *Architectural Digest,* or one of those exuberant lifestyle magazines with tips on raising heritage chickens and canning plums. Only when I turned on the light did I discover, disappointedly, that it was something drier, more demanding: a ten-year-old copy of *The American Oxonian,* a quarterly journal about Rhodes scholars. Volume LXII. I paged through it, past articles like "The Cauldron of Mitteleuropa: Summer 1938," the title alone more potent than any sleeping pill.

So I turned to the index.

At the bottom was a list of scholars who had died recently: all men, all in their eighties. And a woman, a *young* woman.

Lacey Cooper-Reynolds.

1968–1995.

I flipped to the back of the issue, where the actual obituaries loomed like tiny tombstones.

Lacey "gave meaning to the very idea of being alive," wrote the friends who composed her obituary. "If our time on earth can be measured not in years, but in moments of intensity, emotion and adventure, then Lacey lived longer and more completely than any of us could ever hope to."

Yet she took her own life, leaping from the balcony of a hotel in Century City. She was twenty-seven years old, and a newlywed.

I was captivated by the force of her promise, pushing through the seams of every sentence. She flamed into being that night, like a border skirmish or a hologram. I could *see* her, her fierce, dark eyes and rosebud features, chestnut-colored hair falling down her back. I could *hear* her, shouting across the stiffened room at a formal luncheon for Rhodes scholars, when a young man stood and said he was at St. Antony's: "You—I'm at your college. Turn around so I can see your face."

"Brilliant," the obituary said. "Radiant. Beguiling." Clearly this woman was talented and beloved. Why would someone who had everything choose to kill herself? Did she mean to die, or just to send a signal of distress?

On the face of it, Lacey and I had only one thing in common: We were both Rhodes scholars, at a time when there were still few women among our ranks. Like astronauts, we had been launched into a rarefied world, liberating and terrifying, where the view was glorious. But it could be difficult to breathe.

That was true, even now, even in middle age, but there was

something else that bound us. Already I could sense that, subcutaneously. Lacey died only eight miles from where I lived, but some other proximity drew me to her: a sadness, a chaos we could not quarantine.

I looked again at her name: *Lacey Cooper-Reynolds.*

And the date of her death: *July 4, 1995.*

Independence Day, a day of drowsy beauty; the beginning of summer's slumber.

That was the day she chose to free herself.

3.

The next morning I awoke, still thinking about that obituary. The young woman it described was outgoing and exuberant, but also intensely private, happily enveloped by her soft cotton sheets, listening to Jackson Browne. She could command center stage at the most intellectual of gatherings. Yet she also loved to watch *Flashdance,* an iconic bit of Americana that strangely echoed her own life. The contradictions in her obituary were what most intrigued me, but the final contradiction was the most compelling and troubling: that she chose to take her own life—at the very moment she seemed happiest.

A few nights later Michael and I were having dinner with our friends Peter and Lena, who were just back from Hawaii, where Peter was the camera operator on one of the *Pirates of the Caribbean* films.

It was good to see them: Peter, with his jaunty Johnny Depp–like goatee, and Lena, who was compact and caustic, a young Gertrude Stein, but with a better haircut. We didn't get together often, though I couldn't remember why.

Our drinks arrived, and Lena, a photographer, raised her glass. She liked to dominate the conversation, but this time I spoke first.

"Why do people kill themselves?"

"Don't worry," Peter assured me. "They'll bring the appetizers soon."

"No, no! I've been thinking about this girl . . . "

"*Really.*" Peter leaned in lasciviously, and Michael looked concerned.

"She killed herself, this woman. This *young* woman."

"I just read an incredible article about this in *The New Yorker*," Peter said excitedly.

"You did?" Already I was feeling proprietary about Lacey.

"About people who jump from the Golden Gate Bridge. It's a suicide destination."

"The Niagara Falls of suicide," Lena chimed in.

"Most of them jump facing the city. It's a horrible way to land."

"It's all horrible," Michael muttered under his breath.

"But there are people who survive." Peter was growing more animated. "It's kind of incredible. They fall, like, 250 feet and hit the water at 75 miles per hour. And live."

I was amazed. "You're kidding."

"It's true. Like, maybe, thirty."

"Twenty-six," Lena corrected him.

"No, it's more." He scowled at her.

This was an issue for them, the interrupting, the correcting. Maybe that's why we didn't see them more. Every couple has a central issue they keep bumping their heads against, don't they? A challenge that can destroy their love, or certify it.

"The fact is," Peter was plunging ahead, "people who study suicides think most of them are ill-fated."

"No shit," Michael muttered, trying to get the attention of the waitress. She was busy flirting with the bartender, a burly man equally oblivious and inked.

"Most people don't really want to die. It's the classic case of cutting your throat while screaming for help."

"If they don't succeed, most of 'em never try again," Lena added.

"Really?" I tried not to sound too surprised.

"Like those people who throw themselves off the Golden Gate Bridge and survive," Peter went on. "Twenty-five years later, most of them were still alive."

"Ninety-four percent of them," Lena offered. "Or they died of natural causes."

Now Peter was really on a roll. "The point is, suicide is very crisis-oriented. If you can get through the thing you're struggling with, you probably won't try again. People who survive the jump always say that. They realize every one of their problems could have been solved."

"Every single problem," Lena chimed in cheerily.

Peter frowned. "Except one. That they had just let go of the rail."

4.

For days, that conversation continued to haunt me, especially how gleeful Peter seemed in talking of suicide. But most chilling was the image of people jumping from the Golden Gate Bridge facing the city, as if, even in their final moments, they were trying to connect.

Meanwhile Isabel was calling from the next room.

"Mom! Can you come?"

She was working on her "signature" dance, an assignment from her teacher, an imposing African woman with almandine eyes. I didn't know what a "signature" dance was, and I don't think Isabel did either, but she was working feverishly, tracing steps with her toes beneath the kitchen table, trying to choose a piece of music from a pile of CDs.

She was considering Stravinsky's *Firebird*.

"Do you know it?" she asked, ushering me into a chair.

I discovered it years ago, when I was a dancer. But I did not say that.

"Can you watch what I have so far?"

I nodded and curled up on the couch, Emma the dog flopping at my feet.

Suddenly Charlotte catapulted into my lap. "I promise I'll be quiet," she whispered, but Charlotte was rarely quiet, and often what she said revealed, unintentionally, how tenderhearted she was: When her school held a fire drill, she said they had to "evaporate" the building, finding a way, with her misnomer, to save the building, too.

Isabel put on the CD and I expected to hear *Firebird,* but the lilting strains were differently familiar, eerie and evocative.

It was Lennon and McCartney's "Blackbird." Only a young woman was singing it.

Take these broken wings and learn to fly.

The song was tender, melodic, but also disturbing.

Blackbird fly.

I wondered why Isabel chose this as her "signature" song.

Take these sunken eyes and learn to see.

Isabel seemed to drape the music over her like water, unafraid of what was broken, jagged in it. Her gestures were anguished, abrupt—all elbows, all angles.

She looked like she was suffering. Maybe she knew something was wrong in our family, despite the coziness of the cushions, the warmth of the worn rugs. Her father and I were committed to each other, devoted to our daughters.

But sadness had settled over the dishware like a lethal dust. Grief and loss threatened to overtake the house, the yard, sending their tendrils deep into the soil. And no one would suspect such deeply sedimented pain.

5.

Isabel was the reason we'd bought that house in the first place. The *expectation* of Isabel. We were living in a house high in Benedict Canyon, which Michael purchased as a bachelor (mostly because it had a hot tub). It also had sixty-three treacherous steps leading from the street to the front door.

One day, a doe appeared outside the window, her two tiny fawns nibbling at the non–water retentive grasses. I saw it as a sign that Michael and I should have a baby, too. On our anniversary, I declined a glass of champagne, hoping I was pregnant. I was thrilled to discover that I was.

Soon, we had determined that the baby was a girl, and we knew we would call her Isabel. So Michael began calling my growing stomach the "Isabelly." (It was one of those cloying private jokes the newly pregnant share.) But there was no way to lug that Isabelly up sixty-three steps to the front door. Given my propensity for tumbling, it became dangerous, especially in the dark. We longed to live on level ground, but everything with a real yard was too expensive. Everything with a *tree* was too expensive. I was growing bigger and more discouraged by the day. Sometimes, to cheer me up, Michael would sing his version of a song from *West Side Story:*

There's a house for us
Somewhere a house for us,
Peace and quiet and open air
A Frigidaire.
Somewhere . . .

Then one day I happened upon a beautiful place overlooking a canyon, but it was more than twice what we could spend. Michael, ever the negotiator, discovered the empty house was owned by a bank and called, offering half the asking price. We moved in three months later.

We have been repairing it ever since.

Nigel Nicolson once said the best houses have a combination of inevitability and surprise. Ours, inevitably, had an excess of surprise in the number of wobbly structural defects and subterranean leaks. Still, the house was a kind of refuge, sheltered by towering eucalyptus trees that scented the garden. A pair of owls called to each other at night. When dusk descended, crickets chirred like castanets, and I could hear the *yip-yip-yipping* of coyotes. Sometimes I saw them loiter in the street, lanky and diffident. Emma, our dog, pricked up her ears when she heard them howling, in case she was called upon to protect me. She stood ready, too, to defend me from all the babies napping in their strollers, whom she watched leerily from the balcony outside my door.

I had everything I'd ever wanted: love and companionship and the warmth of friends—above all, two healthy, charming children—a dog (although I actually never wanted a dog) and a garden and plenty to read. It was Michael who offered me this: the harmonious peace I thought existed only for other people. The sweetness, coziness, that I imagined in the lighted windows of other people's homes.

But something prevented me from filling out the contours of my presence. I was floating in a spiritual limbo, like a lukewarm bath. My fears swarmed around me like furies, and it took all my energy just to quiet them, contain them.

No wonder I was becoming zombie mom.

Still I tried to fit in, to find interest in the daily rhythms, to seek out color in the garden, variety in the grocery. I devoted my days to the "clucking domesticities," as Virginia Woolf described them: the tending and nurturing and consoling; the defrosting and composting. I knew how lucky I was to have this life, dove-colored and promising. I knew it would fray, even crumble, if I did not nurture it. I would destroy the only thing that had ever given back more than it had taken, that had any hope of rescuing me.

But I was making a mess of it—not a noisy mess, like a drunk at a party, but a slow withering of buoyancy, of belief. The past would show itself, like a gambler's tell, in the way I flinched if someone praised me, or shuddered when I was alone at night, brushing my teeth.

I wanted to live *here,* in the ripeness, abundance, of the present moment.

But the past would not stay put.

One day I lost the keys to the house and I was frantic, searching everywhere, desperately emptying pockets and beating back shrubs. Michael offered to help, and in no time he found them— outside the front door where I had dropped them.

I asked how he knew where they would be, and he answered lightly, "I looked with my heart."

He didn't mean it as a rebuke, but he knew I was floating, hovering, caught between two worlds. I could *see* Michael and the girls, laughing at the dinner table, but the tableau seemed as aspirational, inaccessible, as a stage scene bordered with light.

I could not find my way in.

I could not even find my house keys.

I was not looking with my heart.

6.

The world seemed aqueous, with Michael, a distant point. Cheerful. *Legible.* Looking with his heart. I couldn't *find* my heart, but that didn't mean I didn't love him. I did, and I adored my children. (I wasn't sure about the dog.) But in those days, it was hard for me to feel those feelings. Any feelings. In truth, I was trying *not* to feel. All the while, life was full of sudden jolts and unsuspected longueurs, as if a stage machine had run amok, shifting scenery in a noiseless haze.

Then I stumbled upon Lacey's obituary, and the whole world shuddered on its axis. What made her vaporous presence so powerful? Did she feel as estranged from her life as I felt shipwrecked in mine? I knew so little about her, but our connection felt almost visceral. In her buried heart, I could hear an echo of my own.

Late at night, I would creep downstairs to re-read her obituary, never daring to bring the *Oxonian* upstairs, where my daughters slept.

Upstairs, life was sanguine, peaceable, if predictable. It had nothing to do with the heartbroken writing I could not wait to read: "If you did not know Lacey, imagine Audrey Hepburn in *Breakfast at Tiffany's*: the world was in her spell in public, but in the confidence of friends she was a different person, delicate and vulnerable."

One friend called her "the most likely to succeed among the most likely to succeed, and yet such an unlikely success."

She was funny and fluent and generous, unafraid of the bold gesture or the brazen remark.

No one, it seemed, was less likely to take her own life.

Over the next few weeks, I would find myself thinking of her, wondering if her hair smelled of citrus; if her laugh was low and coarse, like a mischievous boy's. Waiting in line at the bakery or the bank, I kept trying to conjure her. She filled my thoughts, even as I packed my daughters' lunchboxes and tried to ransom my sneaker from the dog.

I wasn't tech savvy, but I took to my computer, hoping to learn as much about her as I could. I turned to the Internet, eagerly keying in names, dates, and details—before this, I didn't even know the word "keying"—looking for any information that would lead more directly to her.

I found an article about her from *The Orange County Register*: a San Clemente woman who invented herself from hard and humble beginnings, juggling a series of low-paying jobs during school and leaving high school early to attend a special honors program at USC. Lacey was active in anti-apartheid groups, and her minor was in peace and conflict studies. I sensed she had not used those skills to soothe herself.

Lacey graduated at twenty with a Rhodes Scholarship to Oxford—one of three world-class fellowships she won. (Another, a Fulbright, she won twice.) According to the article, Lacey first told her mother at age four that she wanted to become a lawyer. She was well aware of the irony of her success, given that Cecil Rhodes, whose will created the awards in 1903, built his fortune on the backs of black African laborers. At age 17, Rhodes left England to grow cotton in southern Africa. He quickly abandoned farming for mining, soon dominating the world diamond market and creating a monopoly with De Beers. Rhodes called the Anglo-Saxon race "the first in the world" and thought "the more of the world [they] inhabit the better it is for the human race." His dream was an intercontinental railroad stretching from the Cape to Cairo, linking British territories in a "ribbon of red." (He also hoped to "recover" the United States as an "integral" part of the empire.) But his most lasting contribution to the African continent was also his most odious: racial laws that became the basis for the system of apartheid in South Africa.

To some, the diamond baron was a murderous colonist, a ruthless oppressor, but Lacey was undaunted. "When it comes right down to it," she said, "the money is to give students a chance to pursue humanitarian goals. If I can change the world because of the money, that will be the greatest irony of them all."

At Oxford, Lacey settled in quickly, embracing life in the city of dreaming spires, transforming the sleepy Oxford University Strategic Studies Group into a high-powered society and perfecting the most flawless rowing stroke on her college crew team. She was the "it girl" Henry James described, who "feels in italics and thinks in capitals," but her lack of pretension distinguished her most: the improvisational ease with which she charmed and challenged everyone she met.

Lacey returned to the United States with a doctorate in international relations, and an additional prize: marriage to Simon Reynolds, who had been her "moral tutor," an irony not lost on her. "She was deeply in love with her husband, a man who represented all she had hoped for in a lifelong companion," her obituary said. "With an Oxford DPhil, she had reached, after much struggle, her ultimate academic goal."

Waiting for Simon to join her in L.A., Lacey began the difficult job of adjusting to the real world, and no world seemed "realer" than Chatsworth & Company, the behemoth management consulting firm. Friends said she did not expect to like the work at first and knew that "better things lay ahead—that all doors were now open to her."

Yet only months into her job, she was discovered facedown in a hotel awning, wearing a business suit.

According to the *Oxonian,* Lacey worried about the tendency for "talented young women to punch so many tickets on the road to success that they easily lose sight of their true personal goals." Her own "true personal goal" seemed covetable but self-contained, a private happiness sealed off from public striving; a world where, for the first time, she could breathe.

Still, even when she had everything she wanted—especially then—she may have felt the accolades were built on a false brightness. Internal demons would prevail. And nothing could buoy her, not even the love of friends, their pain so palpable it was almost viscous. No success could root her in the "real world," stabilize her.

I knew what that was like, to exist in a liminal space, never quite fully situated. To be a person who feels too much, who feels she is not enough. Is that what Lacey felt? Yes, I was casting my shadow over hers, but something within our stories rhymed: the fear. The sense of isolation.

I couldn't help wondering: Why did our paths diverge?

Why did I survive?

But I didn't want to make her death a fetish, to probe it like a rotting tooth. Nor did I want to probe my own past, from which the house beneath the eucalpytus had proved a refuge. From which California proved a refuge: the light and warmth and anonymity and ease. I would cruise down the Pacific Coast Highway in my little brown Sentra, past carpets of beach, Don Henley blasting, *Don't look back. You can never look back.*

Looking back was the very last thing I wanted to do.

7.

Then, to my surprise, I became obsessed with Lacey. Maybe no obsession announces itself at first. But I said nothing more to Michael, fearing that he would discourage me. He was as skeptical of my sudden passions as my runaway fears. He didn't think I should try to invent something called "Mother in a Cup," a line of soups that offered the kind of comfort mothers (supposedly) did. Nor a purse called "the Mother Lode" that would corral all of one's belongings in a single, removable sac. No wonder I felt unworthy of him: I was the "bad" one, who spent too much money or ate fried food. He was disciplined and self-sacrificing.

He was silent a lot, too.

Later, I learned the silence was anger. He was furious, and had been for a long time. He loved me, believed in me, wanted me to be my best self, and a better self to him. But he also watched, leerily, to see how I might screw up.

I think he found me charming and also, to his great surprise, a good mother; in fact, *too much* surprise entered his voice when he complimented my parenting skills. "You're so loving to them," he would say of our daughters. "And supportive. But the best thing is you're not competing with them." I could *never* compete with them. They existed on a different plane, healthy and flourishing, still unformed. And sometimes I would wonder where they had come from. How could someone so damaged make something so whole?

As a young girl, I would lie in bed, as the wallah of the world pressed in, pulling out my eyelashes. Then I began to gouge my face. It was calming, somehow, to carve a hole above my lip, usually on the left side: to defile my face, then hide the mark. My mother noticed the cuts, the rawness, but my behavior irked her. I wasn't happy, but it wasn't her fault. "You think too much about things," she would say, but what she really meant was "you want too much." I asked too much, especially of her. She offered no ballast against my moods, no solace from my insecurities. I was the glowering girl who needed something she could never give.

How could I, who had been scarred, disappointed, and who had disappointed others, make children so fragrant with promise, so free of compromise?

My daughters, goofy in the tub or snuggling beneath my chin, made me hopeful, forced me from my bed. "My friend Mommy," my little one used to cry, at 2:40 in the morning. "Has anyone seen my friend Mommy?"

I had never put those words in the same sentence before.

Yet for someone with my fears, motherhood could seem more challenging—*exhausting*—than performing with the Cirque du Soleil. The level of danger exploded like an oil rig: the stakes were infinitely higher, the perils more acute. That's what prompted my crazy vigil at the bus stop: all life seemed fragile, and harm could come to anyone at any time. The world seemed alive with germs, with threats, with vendettas.

I wanted to raise my children in an autoclave. I wanted to live somewhere immaculate, objects swathed in gauze, each a glittering chrysalis. But my children didn't want that: they wanted to share secrets and sips of lemonade. I would rear back, involuntarily, when they touched my face; the face I had gouged until it was bloody. I thought I was protecting them from something poisonous.

Had Lacey felt that same sense of inadequacy? I once read that people sometimes killed themselves to protect the people they loved. I was still alive, of course, but I was doing my best to protect my family from—well, from *me*. From the way my life leaked sadness like a toxic waste.

8.

~

Despite all appearances, some part of me had always felt insufficient. Not worthless, exactly, but not ambitious enough, controlled enough, *solid* enough. A friend from my Rhodes class was the military aide who carried the "nuclear football," which would have been a terrible job for me, given my tendency to crash into couches and stumble over curbs. Other Rhodes classmates held sway at the State Department. One had pocketed a Pulitzer. (Actually, he won *two*.)

Meanwhile, I had taken myself off the grid, away from cities that seemed gritty and striving, moving to California, where I knew no one, where I had never been. When I first arrived, someone suggested I lash a surfboard to my Sentra to signal that I belonged. But I never belonged. I wasn't a California girl: I didn't own a bikini. I had grown up eating canned fruit and wearing socks to bed. And I was a terrible driver: I borrowed a friend's new Mazda and promptly guided it into the side of a bus. Even the bus driver was appalled. "How could you not see me?" he hollered. "I'm a goddamned *bus*!" Perhaps, in a more concentrated city, I would have been forced to be more intimate. Or maybe, with apologies to T. S. Eliot, this was all the reality, *intimacy*, I could bear.

Yet for someone in self-proclaimed exile, I took a crazy delight in going to Rhodes functions, as if to confirm my unfitness, *otherness*. I'm not sure what I was looking for, but I travelled— to Washington, DC; to Philadelphia; to San Francisco—to find it. Often I had my husband and children in tow.

At one reunion, in Washington, DC, I was carrying Charlotte and two suitcases when I tripped over a woman who'd been a year behind me at Oxford, sitting in the hallway of the hotel.

"I left my breast pump on the baggage carousel," I blurted out, feeling overwhelmed and slightly embarrassed. For some reason, the thought of that little machine circling in perpetuity pained me, as did the cost of replacing it.

"I've got five kids," Margaret said.

"Are they all here?"

"Yes. We drove down from New York. We live in a two bedroom on the Upper West Side. I'm convinced that if we had a bigger place, we'd have fewer kids."

I knew she was an accomplished foreign policy expert. What was she doing now?

"Looking for a bigger apartment in New York."

At another reunion, to celebrate the centennial of the Rhodes Trust in 2003, only Isabel joined me. Michael stayed home with baby Charlotte, and a list of instructions that were an insult to his intelligence: don't put her in a car seat on the hood of the station wagon, don't leave her in the bathtub unattended, don't give her gum.

At the reunion, children were on everyone's mind:

"My daughter's working as my wife's campaign manager," one classmate told me, by way of greeting. He seemed as unctuous as when we first met at the Rhodes regional interviews in 1980.

"How old is she?"

"Twelve." This always irked me about the Rhodes: the feeling that people were awaiting their call from Sweden—or worse, had their children contacting the Nobel committee on their behalf.

But what really bothered me were the actual events at these reunions: lots of talks about unilateralism vs. multilateralism or globalization and the future of employment. Why, I always wondered, did "doing good" have to be defined only in terms of policy? To this day, artists were discounted and women, marginalized, although we were admitted to the scholarship more than twenty-five years ago. In fact, it had taken seventy-five years—and an act of Parliament—to pry open the Rhodes to women, and an air of male supremacy lingered like the leathery notes of a cigar. *Our* interests were addressed, allegedly, by a single panel on how to balance career and family. Hadn't we learned that the question of balance also mattered to men?

So I opted for the panel that was, literally, an afterthought, announced by a little slip of paper thrust carelessly into the program, like the notice of an understudy in a lead role. "Surviving Midlife: The ambitious scholar's quest for satisfaction in a world where there is never enough fame or fortune" was an issue that clearly mattered to men—the room was crowded with them.

Isabel and I found two seats in the back.

"Aristotle was a failure," James O'Toole, a writer co-hosting the panel, said. "His star pupil, Alexander the Great, turned out to be a creep. But Aristotle took on a second career as an advisor to the rich and famous. He was kind of the Oprah of Athens."

James Atlas, his co-panelist, looked nonplussed. He had written a celebrated biography of poet Delmore Schwartz and, more recently, a book about midlife, after being fired from a prestigious magazine when he turned fifty. But he had gotten a book out of it: the best revenge.

"Aristotle thought the experience of reflection was important," James O'Toole went on. "He thought it was something we could do better in the company of friends. It's easier to find one's own virtues in a collegial atmosphere."

"Hence the Rhodes reunion," someone muttered, and I couldn't tell if he was being sarcastic.

"People don't have a shred of an idea who they'll become," another man offered. "There's a guy in my class, a successful DC lawyer, who gave up power and money to do hands-on work in South Africa, to give kids a chance at college or a real job. He changed direction in his fifties to try to find more satisfaction from life."

This, it turned out, was a theme of the discussion: the move from success to significance. Maybe that's why I was here, to find out what happened to all the dreams I had sullied, or was too scared or self-doubting to claim.

"It's all about passion," another man, also in his fifties, said, bristling slightly. "If you're lucky enough to have passion, you're very fortunate."

"It's about the *pursuit* of happiness. Not happiness itself," said another. "The highest good is fulfilling our potential." He turned to James O'Toole. "Wouldn't Aristotle agree?"

"Aristotle would think that a happy life, a complete life, is spent learning, putting your talents to use for your community," James O'Toole concurred.

Someone else interjected, "The Greeks had a word for people who didn't perform public service. Our word 'idiot' derives from it."

Happiness, success, significance, satisfaction. I wondered what Isabel made of all this talk. I looked over, and she was buried in the latest volume of *Harry Potter*.

"Some people have a talent for luck," James Atlas commented wryly when someone mentioned then–Supreme Court Justice David Souter, who was the star of his class. It turned out the word "happiness" comes from the same root as "happenstance." It's all about luck.

And "long alleles" are a genetic component that predisposes people to happiness.

"I have long allele envy," James Atlas said dryly.

I had long allele envy, too.

Yet here were other Rhodes scholars, many noted in their fields, with whom I had something in common: They, too, were trying to triage their regrets. Maybe, like me, they were also haunted by forked paths or shadow selves, by all the things they had failed or forgotten to achieve.

Then James O'Toole let slip someone's name: Stacey. "She was one of our best and brightest," he said mournfully. "She jumped from a building in L.A. Just couldn't handle her success." He was talking about Lacey, although he had gotten her name wrong and also, perhaps, her rationale. Ever the shape-shifter, she was as willing to be used for his purposes as mine. But I didn't know what my purposes *were*. Why was Lacey beckoning to me? Maybe she had something to tell me.

I just had to figure out what it was.

9.

On our way to that reunion in Philadelphia, Isabel had asked, "What's a Rhodes scholar?"

"Someone with a brilliant future in her past," I was tempted to respond. But I didn't say that. I didn't want to seem cynical.

What's a Rhodes scholar? I was probably the wrong person to ask. With no false modesty, I can say I had none of the attributes I, or anyone, associated with being a Rhodes scholar: I was a woman, a writer, a loner, a dancer, a Jew.

The Rhodes, considered perhaps the highest prize for young American scholars, financed postgraduate study at Oxford University for thirty-two students who embodied "excellence of mind, physical vigor, and moral force of character." I never knew how to feel about the scholarship: enamored of its mystique, or cynical about its roots in the exploitation of others; grateful for its generosity, or embarrassed by its self-regard.

Rhodes scholars were meant to "fight the world's fight" with "truth courage devotion to duty sympathy for the protection of the weak and instincts to lead." I didn't have any of those qualities, let alone in one unpunctuated effluence.

And I could never figure out the meaning of "the world's fight."

When I began the interview process as a senior at Yale, women made up a tiny fraction of the applicants. "You're much bigger than your picture," said the man who answered the door at the cocktail party the night before the interviews. *I would* have *to be bigger,* I remember thinking. *My photo was the size of a postage stamp.*

We chatted briefly, and then I asked where the bathroom was. He showed me to a door with MEN chiseled above it. There *was* no ladies' room. He insisted on standing guard outside, his service more begrudging than chivalrous. I could hear him shifting his weight uncomfortably while I peed.

Then he led me to a room, all red leather and Oriental rugs, where other candidates were making small talk in a low roar. The grand room pulsed with a kind of percussive tension: a disconcerting blend of bonhomie and ballistic drive. These were people who could do more than discuss current events: they knew when to laugh loudly or lean in closer for a stolen remark. I expected to be nervous, to be different, but only when everyone looked up did I realize *how* different I was.

I was the only woman in the room.

How could they interview only one woman, when Connecticut was home to so many good colleges, like Trinity, Wesleyan, and Yale? Yale had made a graceful transition to coeducation almost a dozen years before. How could it play host to such a lopsided affair?

The men looked equally uncomfortable in their suits, and I recognized one, Stephen, from the Yale Russian chorus. I thought he should win. Or James, who was an outstanding history student and tennis player. Any of them should win, except me. But I wanted to live in England, to study Shakespeare, to punt on the river, to have picnics, to see plays in production at Stratford-upon-Avon,

Shakespeare's home. I loved tea and scones, but most of all, I loved Shakespeare, newly alive to the complexity and poignancy of his plays. What better way to spend two years than reading all thirty-seven of them (including the disputed ones), even if a "murderous colonist" was footing the bill? After all, the Rhodes was the only fellowship that guaranteed two years of study at Oxford, which had the premier program in Shakespeare studies. And, in truth, I also wanted it for the "pop" of it. Rhodes scholars got their names in *The New York Times*.

The man who had answered the door reappeared with another candidate. A woman! I recognized her as a first year student at the law school. She looked smart and confident, and I hoped she would be easy to talk to. I hoped she didn't expect there to be a women's room—or *women*—as I so mistakenly had.

Even before she shook off her coat, she was being summoned. "If you don't mind, I could use your help," said the man who had opened the door. He waved her over to the bar. "Can you fill these glasses?"

She looked confused but dutifully obliged.

"And maybe you"—he peered down at my name tag; I was growing ever smaller—"could serve the hors d'oeuvres."

When I got home that night, in the diminishing light of late November, I was furious. I wasn't going to let them intimidate me. I knew my chances were slim: I was as unlikely to be chosen as to be named Secretary General of the UN, but I was determined to kick some butt, to loom as large as I could.

The next day, for the interview itself, the door was opened, again, by the man who had guarded the bathroom. It turned out he was the head of the committee, and a former Marine. And I had written a play about Lt. William Calley, who'd been prosecuted for killing dozens of women and children at My Lai. (It seemed like a good idea at the time.)

"You say in your essay you want to write plays for a living," he began. "What if God says you can't?"

"I'll write books," I said, or something equally lame, not even choosing to address the question of God. I was determined not to let them scare me off after the embarrassments of the night before. I knew the Rhodes was the only fellowship that allowed returning scholars to serve on its selection committees. If I won, I could keep others from feeling humiliated as I had.

Later, the head of the committee launched another question, and I remember asking, "Is God still in the room?" And they laughed, all those men. The whole room laughed. That was the moment I won, even if I wasn't chosen to go on to the final round of interviews. I knew I could play their game; I could "pass."

Two days later, I found myself in the lobby of a Boston law firm with the other finalists. We were too exhausted to feel competitive. Some candidates talked about their studies, and many had fascinating, if obscure, interests: fluorescent zebra fish neurons or the political economy of corn. One applicant was so practiced, so polished, the selectors had told him to "cool it." They said he was about to "ooze his way out of a Rhodes." (He was the person I encountered at the reunion more than twenty years later, whose pre-teen was managing her mother's political campaign.)

When the committee members finally emerged, we scrambled to our feet. One candidate was missing. Another had fallen asleep.

"It was a pleasure to meet you all," the head of the committee began. "Please be seated."

Another selector said in a stage whisper, "It was a very difficult choice."

We knew these were platitudes, but they forestalled the inevitable. We searched the faces of the committee for signs of favor or fatigue.

"We're going to read the names of the winners alphabetically," the head of the committee explained, "and we'd like to ask them to stand. Thank you all, again, for coming today."

Then a name that started with *C* was called, and a gorgeous red-haired woman floated up from the couch. I'd noticed her earlier because she was wearing a tight-fitting white dress, while the rest of the women were swathed in voluminous suits. (We might as well have been covered with tarps.) The second name, beginning with the letter *E,* belonged to the unctuous fellow who seemed to have "Rhodes" tattooed across his forehead. (In those days, people didn't brand themselves—in both senses of the word—the way they do now.) The third name was attached to a slight and slightly balding woman, who ended up becoming my neighbor in Oxford and a good friend. My heart sank even as she levitated from the couch. There were only going to be four winners. How could they skip through the alphabet from *J* all the way to *T*?

"Jessica Teich," the committee head announced, and I gasped and sprang up, knocking over a cup of tepid coffee. No matter, the night before the interview, I'd walked into a hook on the back of the bathroom door, appearing before the committee with a huge bandage across my brow.

"You may all shake hands," the committee head urged, and we did. We probably would have stripped naked if he'd asked. We watched as the disappointed slipped away, back to family vacations and final exams. Then he ushered us up a gleaming mahogany staircase into an impressive wood-panelled room.

"Congratulations," he said. "It was a very tough day. You should all be very proud." He launched immediately into a discussion of logistics: "Here is information to help you choose your college. You have to apply, you know. There's no guarantee they'll take you. Some of you might also want to reconsider your proposed course of study. Oh, and there's a phone down the hall, so you can call your families."

The papers in front of us swam with the charming names of academic semesters like "Hilary" and "Michaelmas," with degree programs and entrance requirements. For a moment, I had the spinning sensation of belonging. I had been mistaken for someone optimistic, unmarked.

That shining sense, of being united with something larger, lasted only until I got back to New Haven, in the rain. Right away, people scoffed openly at my selection: One classmate assailed me as I crossed the lawn to the library, sneering, "Why'd *you* get it?"

(It turned out he had been passed over in the first round.)

Years later, at a dinner party, someone suggested I had "slept my way to a Rhodes."

"If only it had been that easy!" I replied.

But the insult stung.

After I was chosen, I would sometimes glance through the annual directory of scholars the way a friend of mine reads cookbooks, late at night in bed, for comfort and sustenance.

I was startled, and often amused, by the names I fell across: archbishops and inventors and explorers of Antarctica. Oh, my. There were several Nobel Laureates, like Sir Howard Florey, who won for the discovery of penicillin, and Sir John Eccles, recognized for his groundbreaking work on synapses in the nervous system. Dr. Eric Lander, pioneer of the Human Genome Project, was a Rhodes scholar, as was Professor David Schindler, whose environmental research led to a ban on harmful phosphates in detergents. There were Supreme Court justices and Olympic gold medalists and at least one country-and-western singer (Kris Kristofferson). Rhodes scholars liked to run things, including—at one point—the Miss America pageant, so the list included a number of prominent CEOs. But the lion's share of luminaries were in government, including a president, two prime ministers, several supreme commanders of NATO, and members of Congress too numerous to count.

Dean Rusk, a Rhodes scholar and former secretary of state, liked to note that there was an unusual number of Rhodes scholars in JFK's administration. "Harvard gets all the credit," he once said. "But Oxford did all the work."

There were also eminent writers, including Robert Penn

Warren, who wrote the Pulitzer Prize–winning *All the King's Men,* and V. A. Kolve, whose book on medieval mystery plays was like a bible to me. On almost every page was someone of distinction, even if obscurely so, like Ivan Getting, who helped create the Global Positioning System. These people seemed to know who they were, *where* they were, and how they had gotten there.

Somehow I had gotten lost.

Most scholars were wired for success—Bill Clinton is just one legendary example—while others like director Terrence Malick shunned the spotlight with equal notoriety, even as he climbed out of the shadows every few decades to direct an Oscar-nominated film. Malick, who once took a twenty-five-year hiatus between projects, made movies a critic called "truly moving pictures of a restless sort. His characters and camera constantly chase and encircle one another, searching for some kind of connection."

Yet the filmmaker himself was legendarily reclusive. Next to his name in the directory were the haunting words: *Address Unknown.*

Other entries, strangely truncated, trailed off in the same spidery italics: *Address Unknown.* Maybe these people jumped ship, or were pushed, by bad luck or wrongheaded choices. Or maybe they didn't want to be Rhodes scholars anymore.

I, too, had spent my years since Oxford running from the Rhodes, away from the spotlight, away from scholarship. I moved to California because I knew no one there, as unrooted in the landscape as the eucalyptus, as alien as the wild parrots calling to each other in the trees.

I wondered if Lacey felt, as I did, like an intruder, undeserving of the opportunity and the acclaim. She was stalked by the specter of failure, of exposure, but no one seems to have noticed. Graceful, affable, she was the belle of her class. Lacey was the "featured" scholar in *The New York Times* piece on Rhodes scholars of her year, but she never believed her own press. Maybe that was the problem.

As one friend put it, she "medicated herself with kudos," but she never felt she was good enough. She was convinced "she had faked her way through life, that none of her accomplishments were real, the praise and accolades were feigned."

I couldn't help wondering: Why did no one sense that she was struggling? Why didn't someone grab her sleeve before she leapt?

Maybe her jump was so decisive, and so unexpected, that no one saw it coming. Maybe no one could have prevented it. Or perhaps they could have, if they had understood how deeply her fear ran, like an icy river, or if they had stopped for a moment and acknowledged their own fear. For it was fear that motivated many of us to compete for a Rhodes in the first place—fear that we weren't good enough, even as we were ambitious to prove we were.

Maybe Lacey, ever an avatar, found herself, again and again, in a world where pressure poisoned her morning coffee, where even the most private moments seemed lit by klieg lights, expectation drumming in her ears. A place where the push to excel was as crushing as an avalanche in the Himalayas; as crushing, and as impossible to escape. She feared, in the words of the Bible verse read at her funeral, that all was vanity. According to her obituary, "Her insecurity was irrational, so it was impervious to all evidence." She felt like an imposter in a world sure to show her up. Like me, she was simply waiting to be found out.

PART TWO

MYTHOLOGIES

I don't know if she is gifted . . . but she is a clever girl, with a strong will and a high temper. She has no idea of being bored . . . Very pretty indeed; but I don't insist upon that. It's her general air of being someone in particular that strikes me.

—Henry James

10.

Days passed, and thoughts of Lacey tugged at me with an almost tidal pressure. I wanted to know more about her, more than the Internet could reveal. That meant venturing outside my comfort zone, but luckily, it did not mean venturing outside my house. I could stay in my pajamas. That was the kind of assignment I liked best.

I would begin by contacting the authors of her obituary in the *Oxonian,* the most lapidary portrait of a loved one I had ever seen. One of them, Todd DeMarco, was listed in the annual directory as head of Human Rights Watch in Washington, DC. That seemed like work Lacey might have loved.

I found his phone number and called in the afternoon, when both my daughters were at school, so that this Lacey odyssey, wherever it led, would not intrude on the little girl sweetness of their days.

Todd was soon on the other end of the phone, and I promptly forgot the dozen or so opening lines I had been rehearsing. All I could squeak out was, "Would you be willing to talk to me about Lacey?"

"I'd be happy to talk about Lacey," Todd responded, but he hardly sounded happy. He sounded rather business-like, even brusque. "Given that it's a serious subject, I probably shouldn't do it while fixing dinner. Call me tomorrow at my office, before five."

In the *Oxonian*, Todd said he was hooked from the first moment he saw Lacey, or rather, from the moment she shouted at him across the strained dining room at the Harvard Club: "You— I'm at your college. Turn around so I can see your face." He had fed her Indian takeout from Moonlight Tandoori, and nurtured her, and withstood her anger when he climbed a mountain in a punishing storm, putting himself at risk without consulting her. According to the obituary, she had trouble forgiving him, but she did, and they grew even closer. He visited her almost every day. He was grateful for his prominence in her "ridiculously crowded" calendar.

Had he been in love with her? He seemed so charmed, but then, so was everyone. Did she have everyone in her thrall? "Charm is a way of getting the answer 'yes' without asking any clear question," Camus said. Did Lacey ever get what she really wanted? What were *her* questions? What was her "world's fight?"

And what questions should I ask of her closest friend? I practiced some possibilities out loud. But there was only one question, really, although I doubted I could ask it: Why did Lacey kill herself?

When I reached Todd, his voice was wary, as if he had steeled himself to talk. I made him laugh with a story about the inflated egos of the people at Rhodes reunions. Then we began.

Perhaps I had lived in La-La Land too long. I expected caterwauls of grief or, at least, a halting recitation. But I forgot that Todd was also a product of the Oxford tutorial system, in which thoughtful disputation is favored over improvisation, cogitation over spontaneity. In American classrooms, students may blurt out ill-considered answers, peppered with personal anecdotes and laced with *like* and *um*. These were throat clearers no respectable don would tolerate.

"When did you last see Lacey?"

A pause. "I hadn't seen her for a while. She stayed behind in England. Then she travelled to Italy and Canada. Japan. She was about to settle down, and her husband was just arriving from England, when she killed herself."

"Why do you think she did it?"

Another pause. "Because she had everything she had ever wanted. And she realized it was never going to be enough."

Todd then told me that Lacey had made a suicide attempt some weeks before, while driving alone at night. Her car went off the road into a hillside canyon. In retrospect, the accident looked like a less than fully committed and thought-out suicide attempt.

"She had terrible swings," he said, emotion tugging at his voice. "She could be extraordinarily charismatic and alive on the upswings. She was a genius at social interaction. No one I've ever known was better at calling attention to herself when she wanted to, at charming people."

He grew quiet.

"She gave little clues to different people," he said finally. "I learned, after she died, that I knew things that others didn't know. Simon knew even less."

Simon, her husband. "Why was he kept in the dark?"

"Because he was her perfect prince. She wanted to keep him as innocent as possible. He was a wonderful guy, very good for Lacey. He just wasn't attuned to the signals. And she would not let him in. Simon was a symbol of a quieter, happier life, but nothing could address her demons. She had just a miserable, miserable, miserable childhood."

"Can you tell me more about that?"

"No."

I wondered at the word "miserable." He said it three times, giving it a thudding majesty. Did that word describe my life when I was younger? Did it characterize my life now? I'd vowed never to be a mother who made her children responsible for her own happiness; who seemed half in, half out of life, as if she had better things to do. Yet here I was, hunched over a cooling cup of tea, grieving for a stranger, while my children frolicked on the floor below. I wanted to join them in their sunny, benevolent spaces—the world of snacks and bikes and books and memos from school. Yet I was as intent on this pursuit as I had been weeks before, waiting at the bus stop, tracking Isabel like a lioness in the tall grass.

There was an awkward silence, as if Todd was considering what to say, not reciting thoughts he had nurtured over many painful years. I wondered again about the morality of compelling someone to relive one of the most horrific moments of his life. Maybe it was time to stop? Maybe he was tired? Or maybe he just needed to take a breath. I had gone from zombie mom to stalker mom to torture mom, all while still in my pajamas. Interrogating a man whose life's mission was to protect others from interrogations like mine.

Then he spoke again. "At her funeral, we all came together to relate our individual experiences, thinking through the 'whys.' I guess you could say there was a more credible narrative, when we brought together everybody's insights. Her story started to add up."

I sensed that he was exhausted, but he seemed to want to go on talking. I asked how he learned of her suicide.

"Our friend Risa called. When I heard, I felt surprise. Well, disbelief. Horror."

"Do you still think about it?"

"All the time. I do think one should keep these things alive. It's common when these things happen for people to tell each other that no one could have known, but I think it's fair to ask what more could have been done. You know, there are two kinds of suicide, classically. One is a cry for help. You do it in a way that doesn't lead to death. The other kind is absolutely designed to end life. You want to be sure that you do it."

"Jumping out a window?"

"Yes. She checked into a hotel and stayed there for two days, over a weekend. It was the Fourth of July, but that wasn't important.

The timing was about beginning a new life. She must have felt that if she was going to do it, she should do it before Simon arrived, so he wouldn't be in the middle of it. He learned about it when his plane touched down. He's remarried now. Lives in London. Two kids."

Todd was silent for a moment. "No one can know what it's like never to have anyone love you. Lacey was totally abandoned as a child, and when she was not abandoned, she was abused. Lacey invented her extraordinary personality entirely on her own, with no help."

"She had no support from her family?"

"None. She was very close to her younger brother. He was her personal project. She protected him. She also had an older sister, who was quite troubled. And her mother—well, her mother was nuts."

"Nuts?"

"Didn't you know? She went to the same hotel as Lacey, five years later, and did what Lacey did. Jumped out a window. Committed suicide."

11.

The image of Lacey's mother following her daughter out the window haunted me for many days. It seemed bizarre but also strangely poignant, conjuring a mother-daughter bond as alien to my childhood as vermouth.

There were great gulfs between my mother and me, like the empty voids into which planes disappear, opaque and sorrowing. Like the scribbled darkness of a child's drawing—the drawing I made as a second grader when Mrs. Emmons told us to cover the creamy white paper with crayon, then slather it with buttery black paint. She wanted us to carve an image out of the trowled darkness, but when I showed the picture to my mother, she said it had "too much black." Her tweed coat smelled damp and woody as she eased herself into a child-size chair, smothering my paper with primer. She had come to school to "fix" my painting for me.

From the time I was very young, I lived a divided life, in a verdant, moneyed suburb of New York. Here oak trees, anthropomorphized by age, bestowed their names on neighborhoods, and the occasional fox darted across the road. The towns formed an icy archipelago of privilege: not just Big Oak, but Laurel Hollow and Lloyd Harbor, where I lived. Sadness clung to the houses like frost: One evening Lexi Toumanoff went out to walk her dog and was found hanging from its leash, her body swinging in the desolate night air. Several suicides followed, including Charlie Dunn, whose sister discovered his body suspended from a tree in their front yard. Every day, when she boarded the school bus in her too-short skirts, we searched her face for answers. She would have been homecoming queen, someone said, if her brother hadn't killed himself.

There was laughter, too, boys playing lacrosse, girls riding show horses, their fathers taking the train to Manhattan to work in finance, their mothers making lunch. In this sunlit world, I was the girl who answered the phone well, who remembered to set the table. But I also felt unseen. So I wandered downstairs to my bedroom, listening to the growl of the grownups in the rooms above, twisting my eyebrows and clawing at my cheek.

We lived in a house my mother had designed—she was one of the few female architecture students at Cornell in the early 1950s—and my bedroom was alone, on one side of the house. My two brothers slept in neighboring rooms at the far end of a very long hallway, with my parents in the bedroom above theirs. It never occurred to me to wonder at my spatial isolation. My mother could not be challenged, her head swiveling on its stem like an exotic Audubon bird. She projected an air of competence, ingenuity, even as I flailed around, falling off beds and stumbling over hydrants. It was no surprise that, when the QE2 disgorged its Rhodes passengers at the end of the five-day voyage, mine was the only suitcase that had burst open, littering the White Cliffs of Dover with my underwear.

My mother was poised and perpetually disapproving, with her chic cap of hair, wearing the capri pants Laura Petrie made famous on *The Dick Van Dyke Show*. Her anger ran cold instead of hot: darker, deeper, smaller than my father's, mixed with disappointment, provoking shame. But once, when I was a baby and wouldn't stop crying, she hit me so hard she had to ask my father, of all people, to make sure I wasn't dead. "Go look in the crib," she told him, "and see if she's still breathing." I don't think she ever hit me again. But she would describe this episode to Charlotte, cheerily, as if it were a bedtime story, or one of the lullabies Charlotte loved.

> *Lula lula lula lula bye bye.*
> *Do you want the moon to play with?*
> *Or the stars to run away with?*
> *Baby, don't you cry.*

Don't you cry. I guess she really meant that. She disliked emotion as much as anchovies or Orthodox Jews. Years later, when she came to see me at Yale, I confessed to feeling desperate, leaning in too close when the New Haven bus blew past. "Do you know what that makes me feel, when you say that?" she groaned.

What about what *I* feel, I wanted to ask. Would I ever get free of this sorrow, to carve my own design?

I didn't want to die. I just wanted to feel better.

Instead it would be death from a thousand cuts, to my brow, my cheek, my chin, my chest, my thigh.

Much later I learned that my mother, too, had suffered. She pined for *sixty years* for the man her parents wouldn't let her marry. Her memory of the day he filled the backseat of a borrowed car with lilacs was more potent than any moment from her fifty-year marriage to my dad.

My parents were an unlikely match, forced together by my mother's parents, even though they hated my father. But they hated the man my mother loved even more. Jan was playful and deft and handsome, an architect, but he was the son of émigrés, political cartoonists. So they forced her to break with him and date other men, or they would refuse to send her to Europe. She agreed.

That summer my father drove up in his blue Chevy convertible. He had hair then, and a devilish smile, and his selfishness had a gleam; it hadn't yet hardened into hate. His rage seemed athletic, and he had promise: he was going to medical school. She could not decide, she said, if she liked him or hated him.

She never did decide. But they married, and that was love for her, someone who didn't read books, didn't know how to say "Gauguin," hadn't been to the Met, didn't know she had been a star student at the Art Students League. He was loud and slim and brash, and he wanted her, so she married him.

But she named her second son Roger Ian. "Ian" is a transliteration of "Jan."

Jan was her soul mate, the man whose whimsical cartoons inspired her to draw little figures on our brown paper lunch bags. She would marvel over his college letters late at night. Still she stayed with my father, in a union as divided as the beds they slept in, pushed together during the day to evoke a temperate domesticity. That was their daylight truce.

Maybe everyone has a second life, a life "running its course in secret," as Chekhov put it. Maybe we are all torn: by the things we want, the things we cannot accept, the things we regret and cannot be reconciled to in our own lives. Part of the act of waking up each morning is the effort to bring these divided selves into focus, bringing our uneasy dreams to rest in our waking selves.

Would Jan have healed the rifts within my mother? Was Michael, my husband, the remedy for mine?

The University of Lausanne once did a study, asking women to choose among a group of anonymous men's sweaty t-shirts. The men represented a variety of genotypes that influenced everything from body odor to the robustness of the immune system. Without exception, the women preferred the smell of the man whose genotype was most *unlike* theirs and would best offset their genetic deficits, from gingivitis to schizophrenia. Michael—fearless about eating food from street vendors—was my genetic deflector, my neutralizer. I could fall asleep at night. My soul was safe.

And maybe, just maybe, Simon was that for Lacey. Todd called him "her perfect prince." She had waited until he was en route to throw herself from the balcony.

The two of them, together for that infinite moment, suspended, united, in mid-air.

12.

The conversation with Todd DeMarco only whetted my appetite— the more I learned, the more I wanted to know. But the process of sleuthing was as alien to me as the Olympic sport of curling. I had grown up in a house of secrets, but I never thought to excavate them.

I'd always felt I was living my life in the margins, as in the margin of a book. Isabel left half-read books open everywhere, flung on couches and folded over the backs of chairs and draped over the lip of the tub. Books, someone once told me, were Isabel's "way into any situation."

For me, they were also the way out.

My mother built a fortress of books: whenever we travelled together, she would erect a seawall of books on the hotel dresser next to the soiled ashtray; dozens of books, even if we were only staying one night. She became a librarian by default, showing up in the local library so often they finally offered her a job.

Night after night, I would find her in bed, tiny night-light clipped to the pages of whatever book she'd borrowed, as my father snored in the bed beside hers, a deep and thudding sleep. She read for hours, head bowed, the sharp angles of her marriage softened by the billowing darkness.

It would have been hard to disturb her in that peace.

For my father, words were a kind of bludgeon: He used the daily terms of his medical practice—"hematoma" and "ecchymosis" and "femoroacetabular impingement"—to intimidate us at the dinner table, describing in gruesome detail the way someone busted his skull falling off a motorcycle, or ripped away the whole length of her arm by reaching back impulsively, catching her sleeve in the motor of her brother's go-cart.

My father was a screamer, his anger provoked by imperceptible transgressions: if there was "too much air" in the folds of the newspaper; if someone had eaten his cherished halvah or dared to disturb him at work. People would tell us that his patients loved him, but I didn't know how they could: He was always yelling at them, too, scolding them for smoking, even as one of his Lucky Strikes dangled from his lips. Day after day, I reached into the pocket of his lab coat to mangle his cigarettes. He could be volatile, brutal, but I didn't want him to die.

My father was a mercurial presence, alternately manic and saturnine. He once told me his favorite poem was ee cummings' "my father moved through dooms of love." I don't think he understood it—I'm not sure I did, either—but I loved that he loved it. In general, he tended toward the stentorian, the grandiose. He could be heard shouting, "I must go down to the seas again" when he was home, which he rarely was. (He adored John Masefield's ode to the mariner's life, but hated to get wet.) More often, when we travelled as a family, he would come up with some tuneful but inane saying—"Oswego, so goes the nation"—repeating it endlessly, like a mantra, like the almond he would savor, turning it over and over with his tongue, long after the candy bar was gone.

My father moved through theys of we,
Singing each new leaf out of each tree.

My father fancied himself a man of words, and he attacked the "Puns and Anagrams" with a delight he rarely brought to Sunday dinners or school events. When I used the word "numinous" in my college essay, he puzzled over it for days, never having heard the word, even doubting it existed.

There was nothing numinous in the lives we lived.

But words were everywhere. My older brother, Douglas, liked to invent new lyrics to the Broadway shows I loved, combining his fascination with Hitler and mine with Lerner and Loewe to yield *My Fair Führer,* with songs like "On the Street Where Juden Live." My younger brother, Roger, was quieter, harder to read. Like my mother, he could draw anything. My siblings were unkind to me, but also to each other: the day Doug realized he would never be taller than Roger—they were arguing over who would ride shotgun in my mother's Subaru—they had a battle that left them both bloodied at the bottom of the stairs.

The atmosphere in the house could ignite at any minute— that was as daily a fact as the delivery of *The New York Times.* When my father turned forty, my mother planned an elaborate party, and she swanned down the stairs wearing electric blue hostess pajamas, the most glamorous sight I had ever seen. My dad, returning home from the hospital, saw her and screamed, "What the fuck are you doing?" Just then, everyone we knew leapt from behind the living room furniture and yelled, "Surprise!"

Like me, my husband, Michael, couldn't wait to leave home: His father was volcanic and sometimes violent. His savvy mother, cowed by so many years of raging, rarely intervened. Our mothers shared a certain superciliousness, combining the hauteur of the high fashion model with the custom official's smirk. Both women were too clever to be kept at home, garroting the roses, touching the iron just to feel the burn.

Michael and I had that in common: homes that were tornadic

in the blasts of anger. Our fathers' rage erupted at the most unexpected moments, bringing with it a vertiginous sensation—the sofa was spinning—but our mothers never seemed to move.

Once, on a family vacation, my brothers were squabbling in the backseat and my father whipped around to pummel them, accidentally slugging my mother in the face. Even then, she didn't move. We just kept driving.

But I still remember the sound of her gasp when his fist hit bone.

The echoes of violence drew Michael and me together, in the way two people can recognize a common struggle, a childhood knot, and help, through their love, to untangle it. Yet there was also a wariness born of our bruising worlds, and a loneliness that sheathed us, isolating us even—especially—from each other; the loneliness that runs deep, a kind of geological despair.

I sensed that Lacey understood this loneliness. I had often driven through the tiny beach town where she was born. It clung to the California coast, halfway between Los Angeles and San Diego, bleached bare by the sun, parched and wanting. There was little to do there other than shop or surf. In fact, I later learned that San Clemente had the highest concentration of surf shops in the world. It was also where Richard Nixon built his western White House, perched high above the San Onofre swells. I went back to her obituary:

> *It sometimes seemed to us that Lacey had invented herself. In a Southern California suburb we saw for the first time, at her funeral, and from which she seemed so disconnected, she created the Lacey we cherished: our most generous, loving, challenging and truly charming friend.*

Lacey knew the high wattage of her appeal, but she also envied her friends their privacy. It was another of the circles she could not square. If she was close to anyone, it was to Risa, whom Todd described as Lacey's "real" sister. Like Lacey, she had come to England after years of juggling school with paying jobs. Poignantly, she, too, considered her time at Oxford "a second youth." Yet they were two women for whom adulthood had barely begun.

Lacey and Risa spent many days picnicking on Port Meadow, where the horses run free, and watching the dark plot of *Twin Peaks* unfold on Channel Four. And they conspired to help Lacey snare the charming tutor at St. Antony's, plotting an encounter after a briefing at the British Foreign Office in London, complete with the perfect Mexican restaurant, the perfect drink. At 1:30 AM, upon returning to Oxford, Lacey called Risa and declared, "I've fallen in love with my moral tutor. What am I going to do?"

"Avoid inappropriate appearances," Risa told her. "Request a new moral tutor. Call back in the morning, when I'm awake."

But reaching Risa proved more of a challenge than I expected. I left a message on her voice mail, telling her I only wanted to "ask some questions about Lacey" for "some writing I was doing." But she didn't return my call.

After a few days, I called again, leaving another message, then another, each more halting than the last.

But Risa never called me back.

I also learned that Lacey had written a book that was now out of print. I went online to see if I could get it from the Strand.

It arrived—dutiful, complete, a work of academic promise, of thoroughness, the beginning of a body of work—and I realized it had been published posthumously, and with some chagrin. Indeed, the horror and hurt of her advisor, Frederick Malcolmson, could be felt in every sentence of his foreword.

Lacey was one of the most stimulating and rewarding
of any student that I have supervised. She distinguished
herself not only in classes and in her essays and thesis

chapters but also as President of the Oxford University Strategic Studies Group . . . on the river, and on the wider Oxford social scene . . . Her sparkle, warm personality, sense of humour and ability to detach herself from Oxford a little, to poke fun at some of its curious ways, all made interaction with her one of the great joys of being a teacher. Sadly with this apparent poise and security in herself went a deeper sense of isolation and doubt about the utility of her work. While she was wonderful in helping others to look at life more positively, she was both hard on herself and stubbornly self-sufficient. When the terrible news came that she had taken her own life, it was so difficult to credit. Someone less likely to have done so would be difficult to imagine.

He insisted that the book was not published because of her death, or the way she died, but because it offered a real contribution to the urgent questions in her field. But his hurt was so evident, it was as if he had gasped upon hearing the news of her suicide and had not taken a cleansing, liberating breath since then. He seemed to ache for answers.

I did, too. But I wasn't making much progress, and when I confessed as much to my friend Janet, she promptly went online and found something tiny and crucial and compelling, something I had missed.

It was the announcement of a 1996 concert by the Los Angeles Philharmonic "dedicated to the memory of close friend and supporter of the orchestra, USC alumna, Rhodes and Truman scholar Lacey Cooper-Reynolds (1968–1995)."

I waited, intrigued more by Janet's avidness than by the information itself. *What,* I wondered, *was revelatory in this?*

"Here it is, at the bottom, in very small print: 'a pre-concert event will be held at 1:30 PM. Rob Lansing, Lacey's voice teacher and music director at Fullerton High School, will conduct his choir in a short concert.'

"Don't you see? Lacey was a singer. I can *see* her singing."

"You can?"

"She gave it up. Like you gave up dancing. She retreated, like you did, into 'the life of the mind.'"

13.

But the "life of the mind" belonged to my brothers, who knew all of Bobby Fischer's moves against Boris Spassky in game six of the World Chess Championship.

When I was growing up, I was more interested in dancing. The center of my world was a ramshackle house at the edge of the water: the Orlando School of Ballet. Vinnie Orlando, who ran it, was a slight man with an imposing nose—he could be funny and insinuating, and he smelled of coffee and cigarettes and sweat. He made beautiful dances to music by Brahms and Satie, and the happiest moments of my day were the moments when he invited me to sit on the parquet floor of the dance studio and watch him work, running his fingers through his long, tangled hair, moving slowly, sinuously, in his jazz shoes.

I began dancing at the age of five; by the time I was ten, I took class every day, then attended rehearsal as a member of the Orlando Ballet Company, performing in parks and theaters throughout New York.

In some ways, I was not unlike the other girls—we were all lanky, with long swingy ponytails. Some had curvier feet or higher extensions. I was known for my jumps. But I knew I was not as talented as the most serious dancers, even as I was more serious about dance than most. For me, it was a kind of escape: here I could be watchful, mimetic, as I could not at home, where no one was watching me.

Vinnie and his wife, Betty, were like characters in a fairy tale: the skinny man with the unruly features and his fat wife. They lived in dilapidated grandeur in a rundown Victorian, with dozens of cats and books by the prophet Seth, a kind of spiritual advisor. I had never seen my parents kiss spontaneously or cuddle, and Vinnie and Betty never seemed to touch. But there was lots of contact between Vinnie and his dancers—the "boys" and the "girls," as they were called—and, as a child, I had trouble telling the difference between what was sexual and what was dancing.

Night after night, I would see the boys—grown men, really—grabbing their partners and thrusting them into the air, or cradling them in lavish plunges. Everywhere I looked there were pliant limbs and charged glances, torsos entwined. In class, too, there were burgeoning bodies, and some girls wielded their power like a poison dart: Nina, the curviest of the dancers, often squatted in class when she was concentrating, and you could see pubic hair through the transparent pink of her tights. Once, when one of the boys had his shirt off in rehearsal, she pretended to suck his nipple. Did women even do that?

I was confused and tantalized.

But over the next few months, as I sat on the floor, long after the other little girls left, and watched Vinnie making dances, I began to realize: the "boys" and the "girls." There was more going on than I thought. Jamie was sleeping with Steve, and Lorna with Chris, and they all lived upstairs in the ramshackle house with Vinnie and Betty. They had huge Italian dinners late at night after rehearsal, when everybody ate and drank and laughed together and cooked.

Once, when I was fifteen, I was invited to stay for dinner, the cats climbing over the dishes, and it was almost eleven at night before the pasta course was served. My parents never let me stay again. Instead, my father would circle by to pick me up on his way home from the hospital, leaning over to unlock the door on the passenger side, as I flung my ballet bag into the backseat, night after night. We never spoke.

The world of the little girls—giggling, pulling on their tights, helping to tuck flowers into each other's hair or darn each other's toe shoes—was a world I didn't fit into. I seemed serious, bookish, compared to them.

And the older girls, living with the boys in the rooms of the tumbledown house, I wasn't one of them, either. They sat on the steps between classes, long legs dangling over the banister, blowing smoke rings and talking about men.

Joe was one of the men they talked about most. He was a dancer, but more athletic, less refined. He was tall and handsome, with a bulbous nose and a voice that seemed high, almost goofy, for a man so muscular. He was always saying lewd things to the other girls.

The summer I was sixteen, Joe began to notice me, tease me, making fun of my name, since his dog's name was Jenny and his favorite song was Donovan's "Jennifer Juniper." "Jennifer Jessica," he would croon, and he invited me to watch him work in the studio, Jenny the dog looking on nervously from the wings. Maybe, he said, he would make a dance for me sometime. Maybe he would make a dance for *us*.

Of course, all the girls wanted that, not just to dance with him, but to feel the smell and stickiness of someone else's body very close. That's what we all wanted most, to be partnered by a boy in a *pas de deux*.

There was a sweetness to it.

Or so it seemed, until the day Joe came up suddenly behind me, lifting me into the air, sliding me down his torso. I could feel him, hard, behind me, feeling me. I didn't know what it meant, but I said nothing.

I felt at home in the gaps, in the silences.

Joe never did choreograph a dance for me. He kept saying he wanted to, coming in close behind me as I stretched in the studio. Soon he was touching me more, teasing me more, wanting me to stay late after class, but not to watch Vinnie work. He wanted to go up to his attic bedroom and talk.

The room was filthy and dark, dance tights and shoes and records strewn everywhere; floorboards sending off splinters; nails poking through walls. There was hardly any furniture: a broken-down dresser; a bed; and next to the bed, a little ashtray made from volcanic rock, bulging and misshapen. I soon discovered that was where Joe kept his joints and his roach clips.

I had never smoked pot before; I had smoked only one ciga-rette with Wendy Masten in the bushes behind her house, begging God even as I did not to strike me down with cancer. I was a "good" girl. But Joe wanted to get high, and when I coughed as the acrid smoke snaked its way inside my body, he laughed and pulled me closer. That was the first time we kissed.

I didn't want to kiss Joe, even though he had beautiful lips, shaped like small balloons. I wanted to get away from him, back downstairs to the dressing rooms or the barre. But soon he was kissing my neck, my head bending down to make room for his kisses; he was pulling me onto the bed, on top of the soiled sheets. Soon he was feeling the place where my breasts were just begin-ning, reaching into my tights to put his hand somewhere more private, where no one's hand had been.

Day after day, I followed him up to his attic room, no lon-ger watching rehearsals, no longer studying the older girls as they stretched or flirted with boys. I didn't fit in with the little girls, but neither did I belong with the big ones, who knew how to suck a man's nipple, who could do a full extension while reaching down for their coffee in a Styrofoam cup from the deli across the street.

I belonged with Joe.

I grew used to the rancid smell of the attic bedroom. Jenny the dog grew used to me. She would settle at the foot of the bed, eyes flashing, as Joe laid me down, too close to her, and began to fondle me, stroking my arms, my breasts, reaching between my legs.

I didn't want him to touch me. I didn't want to touch him.

Really, I just wanted to go home.

But I could not give it up: Here was a man whom everyone noticed, who noticed me. A man who wanted me. And I wanted that.

"Why won't you kiss me?" Joe would ask, as the weeks became months, his frustration like a clenched fist.

Because I don't love you, I wanted to say. Don't people just kiss the people they love? I was waiting for that, even though I didn't know what that would feel like. I imagined it as different, somehow, from the sweeping, surging feeling I had when I was with Joe; when he would wriggle my leotard past my hips, tugging off my tights; when he would shove his hand inside me, fingers moving. He wanted me to move.

What he wanted, most of all, was to make love to me. I didn't want that. I wasn't ready for that. I was curious, but for someone my age, like Bobby Sullivan, who had a mustache that was just beginning, who looked down at his sneakers when he wanted to tell me something, who was part of my life at school.

Here in the attic, the floor littered with dirty dance tights and the stubs of cigarettes, I knew I wasn't safe.

But at least I wasn't hovering, vaporous and disembodied. I was somewhere where someone wanted me.

"I want you to fuck me," Joe would say, his voice husky with longing.

"No," I would say.

But my body was saying something else. My body was moving with his body, even as I was protesting, trying to get away, even as Jenny the dog circled on the rug, never settling down.

"I want to fuck you."

"I have math homework."

"I'm not good enough for you, is that it?" Now he was sneering. "Little missy from Lloyd Harbor, with the big, fancy houses and the tennis courts."

"Joe, this is crazy. I shouldn't even be here. I shouldn't be doing this."

"Why not?"

"You're almost thirty. We could get in trouble."

"Yeah? Who's gonna know?"

"I could tell someone."

He reached past me, brusquely, for a joint on the lip of the ashtray.

"I could tell my parents."

"You fucking tell them, and I'll kill you. I swear I will."

He inhaled the joint and his voice softened. "I just want to fuck you. I want to make you feel good."

He moved in to nuzzle me. "Jennifer Jessica," he started to croon.

"No." I pushed him away.

Anger suffused his face like lava, flowing over his features, narrowing his eyes. I had seen that look before: on my father, when I fell and broke his camera in Sequoia National Park; on my older brother, when he pushed our cat off the top of the stairwell to see if she would land on her feet.

Now Jenny the dog was whining, and Joe swung at her, but she ducked away.

Wham! His knuckles landed like a caterwaul against my cheek.

"Bitch. Don't push me. Don't ever fucking push me."

"Joe—"

He grabbed me and smashed me against the bed railing. "Don't fuckin' push me. Don't you ever push me."

"Joe, I'm sorry." I started to cry.

"Who the fuck do you think you are? You fuckin' cunt." He slammed me against the wall, so hard the shutters shook.

Now I was really crying, and Jenny the dog was whimpering, eyes lowered, ears flat to her skull.

That's how it began, and soon the beating was as frequent as the caressing.

As frequent and as inevitable.

Before long, Joe was coming to my parents' house at night, slipping through a door that led outside to the pool, where a family of geese nested, to my father's dismay. No one ever swam in the swimming pool but the geese. Joe pushed his way in, his cheeks inked by the cold, his nostrils glistening. He had ridden the four miles on his rusted bike.

He would throw his battered leather bomber across my desk.

"It's cold out there," he said, nuzzling me. "C'mon, baby. Warm me up."

"Someone will catch us, Joe."

He murmured into my neck. "And then what?"

I didn't know.

"You can't keep doing this, Joe."

"Yeah." He was nibbling my shoulder. "That fuckin' bike. When I get some money, I'm gonna buy Chris's Camaro. I'll take you somewhere for a drink or something. I mean, when you're older. I'll dress you up all fine."

He reached beneath my nightgown.

"You'll be hot . . . "

"Stop it, Joe."

"You don't want me to stop it. You know that."

* * *

Why didn't I ask someone for help?

When I came home from ballet with a welt, I invented a mishap in rehearsal. When I got an infection, I blamed a tampon or the close-fitting tights.

Why did I let it happen?

Because, before I knew it, it was happening. He had hardened against me, and he would not let me go. He was *on* me, swallowing my mouth, my neck, my shoulders, swallowing my freedom, hanging my hair from his fingers like a flag. We never actually made love, and that was largely the problem: Joe knew he would never "have" me, and I could not tell him why. I know now that I was waiting, waiting for a reason; soon I had lost so much, the reason had to be real. I was waiting to be found out or to fall in love or to be persuaded. But the violence became the reason not to give in.

"No, I won't sleep with you. I'm too young."

"No, I don't want to."

"No," and the fists that followed became my life.

I know that the violence shapes you, claims something in you, changes its name. Puts its mouth on you. You can never go back. The chaos, the drama, grabs at your thigh, like a thistle tearing into flesh. Threads its way between your teeth and tongue, like a horse's bit. From the moment it begins, it declares itself as something welcome. It is brutal, beckoning, but familiar, too. I was drawn to Joe, to his beauty, his goofiness, his desire for me, but there was something more. I was grateful to be recognized. To belong.

In the moments before it begins, there is a kind of anticipation, as before an earthquake. Objects shudder. A dog may stir. You tremble; you brace yourself, but there is also a kind of ecstasy. You can make this happen. You can do *this,* too. There is pleasure, because there is clarity, in the brutality. Everything else seems puny, compromised. If you can survive this, you are stronger—well, maybe not stronger, but more unafraid. Nothing will penetrate. Not grief. Not sex. Not sleep.

You have surrendered the part of yourself that is most tender. Why do you give that up? Why give that part away? Because, at least at first, the violence curls up inside you, where you have not been reached. The man who beats you may seem to be holding you. You know how dangerous he is—or you *would* know, if you could find that part of yourself that was sentient, but that part was dulled, dissipated, long ago. You try to stand up to him, like the time a classmate, David Silver, came to a dance performance. But it was Joe who prevailed, as he always did.

"Tell him to get lost," he growled, grabbing my arm roughly. The stage makeup exaggerated his features, making them seem grotesque. He had drawn spikes around his eyes to emphasize them, but they only accentuated the feeling that he could explode at any moment. That was Joe: a grenade with its pin already pulled.

"Who?" I said, wrapping the satin ribbons around my toe shoes.

"That asshole." The park was empty, but for the person Joe was gesturing at. "What's his name?"

"David."

"David who?"

"David from school."

Now he was smirking. "That's his *name*?"

"No. It's Silver. I think."

"You don't know? What the fuck is he doing here?"

"I don't know. I didn't ask him to come."

Joe leaned in so close I could see where he had tried to contour his nose, to little avail. He still had traces of lipstick on his lips. "Really? The punk shows up, just like that, for *An Evening of Ballet*. Stop bullshitting me."

"I'm not, Joe. Please. I gotta go."

"I don't see your dad's car."

"No. I'm . . . David's driving me home."

"Are you kidding? You didn't know he was coming, but he's driving you home?"

"Joe . . . I'm sorry. Please."

Just then, David approached, mop of hair obscuring his eyes, his hands shoved deep in the pockets of his stoner jeans. He was a lacrosse player with a lopsided pirate's grin. I really *didn't* know him well. But no one had ever asked me about my dancing until he did, and it was a big deal for him to borrow his parents' car and call the box office to reserve a ticket. I thought he was smart and *seriously* cool.

"Hey, Jessica," he said.

"Hey," I said, walking to the edge of the stage.

"How you doing?"

"Good. Thanks for coming. Did you like the show?"

Suddenly Joe rose up out of the darkness behind David. "Hey man, you don't belong here," he snarled, rage blooming in his face. "You should leave."

David looked startled. "No, I'm okay. I'm good."

"No, you're not, man. You're in my way."

He shoved David into the folding chairs, the makeup on his hands leaving prints on David's t-shirt, with its picture of a humongous tongue.

"Joe!"

David staggered backward, but didn't lose his balance. "Hey man, this is a public place," he said quietly. His voice had a low and very appealing rasp.

"No, it's not, you punk. It's *occupato*." Joe liked to use—or misuse—grandiloquent words.

He swung at David, barely missing his eye. "Beat it before I bash your head in."

I gasped as David reeled.

"Joe—"

"I said 'beat it.'" He leaned in as if he might swing at David again. Then he hoisted himself onto the stage with one hand and disappeared into the wings.

David bent down to pick up his car keys, which had fallen, then rose to face me. He looked more sheepish than stunned.

I wanted to say "hey, what a crazy first date" or something, but I was tongue-tied. Besides, I didn't know if it *was* a date. It certainly wasn't a date *now*.

"I've got practice in the morning," David said. "I gotta get going."

"It's okay." I shrugged. "Don't worry about it. Go."

After that, Joe grew bolder, showing up at my high school during lunch period, pounding on the window, gesturing to me. The lunch monitors would wave to me as I walked out the door, clutching my lunch in a paper bag, my name written on it in my mother's architect hand. I would climb into a beat-up VW that belonged to Vinnie, Rod Stewart's "Maggie May" blaring on the radio, and we would drive across the street to an empty field. Joe would molest me, Jenny the dog slouching in the backseat, and I would will myself to think about math class, or whether David Silver would ever speak to me again, his mouth part-grimace, part-grin.

I'd hoped David wouldn't tell anyone what happened at the performance, even as I hoped he would.

Maybe if he had, someone would have intervened to stop Joe, to question him at least. Once, on the stairs leading down to my bedroom, my mother called out to me, "Where did you get that bruise?"

"At dance," I replied softly. I wanted to tell the truth. Maybe she could sense that there was more to the story? I wanted her to know I needed her, even before I could say it, just as Isabel did now.

"Be more careful next time," she warned, never stopping to examine the welt, more compelled by the dirty dishes or the dog.

"I will." I'm not even sure she heard me.

But I didn't know about "next time." I feared the next time, or the next, I would be dead.

Then one day, I marched through the kitchen door (rather than *into* it, as I sometimes did) and announced, "I want to go to Paris."

"What?" My mother was incredulous.

"I want to be an exchange student in one of those college programs."

"But you're in high school," my little brother chimed in. "And you don't speak any French!"

"I'll study mime or something." I knew it sounded ridiculous. "I'll learn another language. Finally."

But the language I needed to learn was the language of how to tell them: I'm leaving because I'm afraid. I'm leaving because sometimes Joe hits me so hard, I can feel my brain rattling, like a penny in a dish. I'm leaving before it's too late to get out.

I had never been on an airplane alone, but I flew to Paris to live with a very strict family, in the shadow of the Eiffel Tower, in a tidy bedroom with a tiny bed. The neighborhood, in the fourteenth arrondissement, had none of the charm of the Ile St-Louis, but I loved that it was a real place, of working people, although I could never figure out exactly what Monsieur Pasquier did, other than take sudden, solitary trips to the country, returning with large clouded bottles of his homemade calvados.

Madame Pasquier was elegant and commanding, her eyes the pearly grey of the Parisian sky, her hair swept up in a magnificent swirl. But she could be cruel, too, impatient with Asha, the Moroccan woman who rarely left the little kitchen, whose couscous was an exotic evocation of another world. Madame Pasquier prepared my first meal, a rabbit, complete with its roasted, shriveled head, which she presented to me, the guest of honor, like a prize. Their daughter, Christine, was as blonde and round as I was dark and gangly. She hated me and refused to speak to me in the little English she knew.

For the first month, the Pasquiers sat me in front of the television, and I did little else but watch newscasts and game shows and soap operas, until such time as I could come to the table (Madame Pasquier would call us with a brisk "à table!") and join the conversation.

The Pasquiers seemed to enjoy my company, and I made them laugh with my absurd mistakes in French.

They were touched, too, I think, by my dutifulness: when I forgot my key one evening and didn't want to disturb them, I spent the night curled up on the mat outside the front door.

Mostly I didn't come home late. I didn't forget things. And when Jean-Christophe, their nephew, flirted with me at the formal Sunday luncheon, I could flirt back, in my faltering French, never worrying that something bad would happen. The Pasquiers made certain it would not. And though I was American and Jewish, I felt strangely at home in my otherness.

I could finally breathe, wandering the rainy streets, unaware of their glamour, happy to be away, anonymous. I spent hours in the Jeu de Paume, absorbing like sun the ravishing paintings: the indiscretions of the Toulouse-Lautrecs, the rosy inanity of the Renoirs. Degas's dancers had an insouciant charm, although their poor technique always irked me: the limp arms and sickled feet, the distractedness. More soothing were the Vermeers in the gallery across the park, the maidens' faces flooded with light. Often there was a man—a tutor or music teacher—counseling the young woman, but his back was turned to the viewer, his visage effaced. In this world, men were solicitous and consoling—they were *Flemish*—they did not tower over women, obliterating them.

Years later, I brought Isabel to a traveling exhibition in New York for a reunion with those paintings. I loved that Isabel loved looking at paintings as much as I did. That day, she was transfixed by

Constable's creamy study of a girl, *Mary Freer*. Its subject was tender and searching, looking out frankly from the canvas, even as Isabel looked in. Finally, after she had been standing there for what seemed like hours, a guard leaned over and whispered, "I would *give* you that painting if I could," and Isabel blushed and moved on. But the afterimage remained: two figures, teetering on the brink of adolescence.

That is the moment smart girls can be swallowed whole.

Is there a single moment in which we are forever altered, leaving behind the person we were; a moment to which we can never return? Like the moment when Joe first lifted me, so high I could no longer see myself in the mirror. I could only see the other girls, laughing, chatting at the barre. When he put me down, the spot where I'd been standing had vanished. And the girl I was? She had vanished, too.

Did Lacey suffer such a moment, an event that sent her spinning away from her center of gravity?

Would Isabel, too? How could I protect her from an instant, an incident, that traps her, freezes her, disuniting her image and its negative; a moment when she loses her bearings, her sense of who she is. I wanted her—both my daughters—to remain whole, intact, concentrated, immune to ridicule, to injury, intent only on what they believe in. Was that kind of integrity even possible? Maybe not, but I couldn't help feeling envious of Constable's young subject, safe behind glass on a museum wall. Envious that there was someone standing guard.

14.

❧

But my daughters were safe, weren't they? Safer than I was. Safer than Lacey, too. They were having lovely lives in peaceful, congenial spaces.

Then one day Isabel asked, "Are you happy?"

And I felt the polar ice caps reverse.

I shouldn't have been surprised. Wasn't I wondering the same thing, when I was Isabel's age, about my own mother? There was only one difference: I'd never have dared to ask.

"I'm happy you're here, and Charlotte, and Daddy," I could have said. Nothing had ever been truer. But I knew that wasn't what she meant.

"Mommy, are you happy?" she asked again. Why was she asking? Perhaps she could not be happy unless I was.

I wanted to tell the truth, as I always had, even when it was inconvenient. When all the other mothers told their pre-schoolers that the classroom pet had gone to hamster heaven, I did not lie. But, since I'd first found Lacey, a desperate truth was beginning to dawn on me, one that I could never share with Isabel: I didn't know what happiness meant. I "knew" the idea of happiness from books, like the culminating dinner party at the end of *To The*

Lighthouse, a radiant scene filled with all the love and comfort the central character can provide. She is a woman "so boasting of her capacity to surround and protect there was scarce a shell of herself left for her to know herself by." That was a feeling I better understood, that lack of self-knowing (and the convoluted syntax).

I didn't know how happiness felt.

That night, I dreamt about a baby falling from a table. I didn't know the baby. I didn't even know I was having a dream. The baby was falling, and I could not catch her. I startled awake, shaking and disoriented.

Freud—and my husband Michael—would probably say *I* was the baby. But, sadly, the baby was Isabel. Or had been: she really had tumbled from the changing table, as I bent down to grab a diaper from the shelf below. The whole thing took place in slow motion, as if underwater, and somehow—maybe it was that dancer's training—I knelt down in time to cradle her tiny head in my hands. For years, I thought that was the worst thing I had done as a mother. I thought that was the worst thing a mother could do.

But I had been looking away all this time, while Isabel was suffering. When I saw the anguished dance she created for school, to the strains of "Blackbird," I knew.

Take these sunken eyes and learn to see.

I remembered that, in pre-school, Isabel insisted on being called "Dolores."

"Is that her middle name?" Jolene, the amiable teacher, asked.

"No, her middle name's Marguerite. We thought, if she needed a nickname, we would call her 'Daisy.'" ("Marguerite" was the French word for "daisy.")

Jolene smiled knowingly. "She's no Daisy."

"She's no Dolores either," I shot back.

"Don't worry, you can always call her 'Lola' when she grows up," Jolene reassured me. "But 'Dolores' is okay with us."

It was one of those progressive pre-schools, moms in their

Lululemon pants, dads discussing their weekend grosses. *Everything* was okay with them.

In that moment, I had that sensation that overcomes new mothers like a sudden bird of prey: my child was a stranger to me. Yet I felt I had known her so deeply, completely, even before she began to talk. At the time I wondered, *Why do toddlers even* need *language?* I already felt so close to her, bound to her, besotted with her.

Months later, I was searching her little clapboard bookshelf for something to read her as she went to sleep, even though I knew she would go on "reading" long after I turned out the light. Next to *Where the Wild Things Are* and *Harold and the Purple Crayon* was a book I hadn't remembered buying: *Going Home,* about a little girl whose parents return to Mexico to work, leaving her and her siblings behind. She worries, this little girl, that she has been abandoned. Will she ever see her mother again? It turned out this little girl was named 'Dolores.'

From the Spanish word "dolor." For "pain."

Here was Isabel, anxious, perhaps, that her own mother was abandoning her. Had she been wondering, agonizing, all these years? I once read that daughters worry more about their mothers than mothers worry about their daughters, which seemed inconceivable, given my crushing anxiety about them. I never wanted them to worry about me.

Charlotte gave me a poem:

Mom
I love the way you laugh
When I look at you
I think of bright colors
Like yellow and green
I wonder what you were like
When you were a little girl

I loved that she saw me laughing. That she associated me with bright colors. But she wondered what I was like as a child. Would I ever tell my daughters what happened all those years ago? I hated that it hovered over them, like a malevolent gloom.

Suddenly, I *knew:* It wasn't enough just to take them to swim practice and ceramics; to wait for them at the bus stop, reading the crumpled arts section of *The New York Times;* to be the mom other mothers chose to host their children on playdates; to watch over them while they swam. I was good at being a mom, and there was nothing that mattered more to me, but I felt like a child's drawing, a skeletal outline of a mother, empty inside. But I wasn't empty. I was full of truths I wanted to tell, love I wanted to lavish, especially as Isabel edged closer to the age I was when I met Joe.

"Dénouement," Isabel once said, when asked her favorite word. She said it meant the unraveling of a knot. Meanwhile the past—*my* past—was tightening like a noose around her neck. Until I freed myself, she could not be free. I needed to unravel this knot, of longing and betrayal, woven in secrecy, so I could love my daughters, so I could liberate them. Now, at last, I knew why Lacey beckoned.

Lacey was the key.

15.

"I need to hire a PI," I told Michael as he was brushing his teeth. I often ambushed him when he was standing at the sink.

"What?"

"I need to find someone. Find out more about her. I need to find her siblings, if I can."

"Wait a minute. I can't hear you." He turned off the water. "What?"

"I've been thinking about that woman."

"The one you told Peter and Lena about?" It had been weeks since our dinner with them. Michael seemed surprised that I was still thinking about her.

"Yes. Her name is Lacey."

"That's a weird name."

"Well, she has an even weirder story. I think. I don't know a lot about her."

"You know she killed herself. Isn't that enough?"

"I want to know *why* she killed herself."

"Why do you want to know?"

"I don't know." I wasn't ready to explain that, in my mind, Lacey had become tied up in the need to keep our daughters safe. "I won't know until I find out more about her. Does that make sense?"

He thought for a moment. "No."

But the next day, beside my toothbrush, was a business card with the name of the private investigator Michael had used for clients: FRANK McCULLOUGH, PI.

I called him right away and was pleased that he seemed to have the requisite Robert Mitchum–like mumble. But his first words were staggering: "If she were alive, this would all be moot."

"She's not," I shot back, but he sounded so sure, so dramatically undramatic, I was a little spooked.

I'd never spoken to an investigator before. Did he know I was wearing my pajamas? I tried to imagine him: rumpled; grizzled; fingers nicotine-stained; divorced, maybe, with a daughter, whom he rarely saw, whom he hardly understood. Probably wearing a day-old shirt. Did he have a revolver? Did they even call them "revolvers" outside a Bogart film? No, no, no: this man resisted being romanticized. Resoundingly. Michael, ever prescient, knew the kind of person I needed next. A skeptic who could lend gravitas to my inquiry, my quixotic endeavor: dusting for the fingerprints of a ghost.

"How do you know she's dead?" he persisted.

"I know people who attended her funeral," I told him. "Her good friends, from when she lived in England."

"Would it be helpful if I could get you the death certificate?"

What would I do with a death certificate? "Yes."

"Send me the obituary. And $200. I'll get started on this." He paused. "I've just looked these people up on the Internet. There's nothing."

"These people." "Nothing." It was as if that were his estimation of them.

I was silent, waiting for him to say more, trying not to fill the awkwardness with my awkwardness. Then he spoke again.

"I haven't worked on it yet, so I don't know how it will turn out."

"There's nothing you could find that wouldn't help."

I watched my email for days, waiting to hear from him, wondering if his communication digitally would seem as dry. A week or so later, he sent an email saying to await some development. "I'll have something for you on this case by the end of the day."

He had the last known addresses for Lacey; for her mother, Lorraine, and stepfather, Robert; and for her siblings, Corinne, Linda and Kyle. In bold next to her mother's name, it said "Death." She had been sixty-one when she died. But next to Lacey: nothing. And, falsely, it gave her age, thirty-seven, as if she had survived another ten years. As if she were still alive now.

It was an oversight, of course, but it felt somehow fitting: a testament to the lingering presence of a woman who loomed so large. Maybe Lacey didn't want to be less than she had been thought of, less than she'd promised everyone, even from the pages of *The New York Times,* that she would be. She is a mirror image of all those who stay, who settle, who try to find meaning in a life that doesn't surprise or soar. This lesser life, which perhaps signals maturity, has its pleasures, but also its promise betrayed.

PART THREE

SHADOWS

One need not be a Chamber—to be Haunted—
One need not be a House—

                              —Emily Dickinson

16.

Knowing the names of Lacey's family grounded my search; the way an electrical charge is grounded, the earth providing a reservoir, a common return. They would know the forces that shaped her, the soil that nurtured her. But would they want to share that information with me? After all, I was a stranger; a stranger in pajamas. Holed up in an attic office. Stalking a ghost. That ghost was their *sister*, whom they had loved, for whom they grieved. Or so I imagined. I had to be ready to be accosted or challenged or dismissed.

"How'd you find me?" Lacey's brother, Kyle, responded to the message I left on his answering machine.

I told him I had gotten his number from a private investigator.

"It's been ten years since she died," he acknowledged. "Eleven in July. Independence Day. Did you know that?"

I told him what I had learned so far, including the names the PI had given me. It turned out Linda was his ex-wife, not his sister. Luke and Patty were half-siblings from his father's first marriage. He dismissed them all as insignificant.

And Corinne, his full sibling?

"I'm still very close to her. She just moved to Maine a few weeks ago. She lives with somebody." He thought for a long moment and almost laughed. "I'll let her tell you that part of the story herself."

Before we talked at length, he wanted to know more about my "motives." I told him about my time at Oxford, about my daughters, about a book I had written on raising children.

"Look, I'm not gonna make you dance on eggshells," he said kindly. "It's been a long time since anyone's asked. I had several requests for interviews. I turned them all down. No one's asked for about five years."

Quickly, tenderly, Kyle revealed himself, wry and wounded, stricken but steadfast, a survivor. Later I would wonder, what made him trust me? Was I really trustworthy? Or was it because I hadn't done a very good job of protecting myself? Maybe what it really means to be a survivor is to be able to talk about the pain, but to feel somewhat removed from it. To acknowledge it—even the lurid, or as he would later say, "absurd" elements of it—but to let it rest at a distance, contained like a serpent in a jar.

"You know, there's a misnomer in society," Kyle told me. "People always ask, 'Why did someone do it?' Is there a singular trigger? I don't think so. I think the human psyche is infinitely more complicated than that."

He paused for a moment, his focus becoming more personal. "My sister wasn't damaged goods. She was very scared. Because of her success, she became a trophy, including to my family. The expectations were too much . . . "

Lacey, he said, worried endlessly about Chatsworth, the consulting firm where she was to start working. She would no longer be "the smartest person in the room." And they paid her a lot of money, more than she'd ever seen, but she didn't really care about money. She cared about Simon, wanting to make him happy, now that he was leaving his job and family, his *country*, behind.

"You know, everybody treated her like an icon," Kyle went

on. "She was very, very successful, and everyone wanted to emulate her. But she started to lose weight. She displayed a lot of self-doubt about her ability to do the job."

I wanted to ask what that job was, but I knew Chatsworth put a high premium on confidentiality. I was not surprised to learn they employ more Rhodes scholars than any organization but the CIA. Kyle told me he thought his sister worked for the Los Angeles Philharmonic, but she could never actually disclose her assignment. Why would working for an orchestra have exerted such pressure on her?

"The pressure she felt was greatest from those closest to her. She was so successful. Charming. Smart. But she'd say, 'I'm so scared. I just want to sit down on the couch, have a glass of wine, be a normal person.' Everybody was so proud of her. She was afraid of letting them down."

I was struck by his use of the word "normal." Did Lacey feel he was one of the people she had to impress?

Curiously, Kyle told me: "Lacey was always very apologetic for all of her success. She spent very little of the money she earned. At one point, she said, 'I've always wanted a Saab.' I urged her to buy it, but she was stubborn: 'I could never do that.' She bought a Toyota Corolla instead."

I stumbled, listening, not sure where to direct him. I expressed dismay at all he had gone through and tried, feebly, to ask a question that would lead him directly to her. "What was her voice like?" I meant the texture, the pitch.

"It wasn't pretentious," he said to oblige me, perhaps uncertain of what I meant. "Her diction was very articulate. At other times, she sounded like she was off the beach in San Clemente. She was a horrible speller," he said and laughed. "She wasn't full of herself, far from it. She was very real.

"Once when she hired some movers to move her stuff into her apartment in Westwood, she said, 'The little men are getting there . . . ' Then she looked horrified. 'I just referred to them as *little men.*' She was afraid someone would think she was this stuffy, arrogant . . . " His voice trailed off.

I, as ever, reverted to my fallback position, poking fun, but affectionately, at the Rhodes. "Nothing could be stuffier," I said.

"She was proud of being a Rhodes scholar. She could have been president, if she'd put her mind to it, but she didn't have a killer instinct. And she didn't think she could do the math. I was taking calculus at the time, and I remember reassuring her, 'They're not hiring you to do the math.'"

There is something of the little brother in that statement: trying to comfort her, while perhaps misunderstanding her fear. Yet he said he had never been closer to her than in the weeks before she died. "We became isolated by life, but we came back together as we got older. Our last meal together is one of the fondest memories of my life."

Lacey had called to say she wanted to see the video of him performing in a high school play. *A high school play?* Even Kyle thought it was strange, since she had seen the video "a thousand times." But he welcomed her with the best bottle of wine he had. They sat on the couch, sipping red wine "like normal people"— that word again—"not trying to impress each other."

And she told him she loved him.

Only later did he realize: "She was saying good-bye."

She couldn't do the math: add up the expectations, the way that success beckoned to her, even as she belied its importance, even as she wished to sit on the couch "like a normal person" and watch TV. Have a glass of wine, joke with Kyle, watch his video, while outside the window, the darkness exerted its own gravitational pull.

17.

Like *a normal person:* That was the phrase that dogged me late at night. What did it mean to Lacey, and to me?

I, too, wanted to seem normal, but I never felt I was. Maybe we are all double agents, incognito in our own lives. On the surface, we seem fine; *more than* fine, we seem cheerful and competent. Then we find ourselves stalking our children on their way to ballet.

I had stumbled away from my parents' home to live in Paris, then to study at Yale, aware always of the difference, the falseness, between who I seemed to be and who I was. Maybe Lacey felt this, too, when she arrived at the University of Southern California, where she was on scholarship. Maybe she worried her financial status was somehow telegraphed, tattooed on her forehead. She may have felt out of place at what was then known as the "University of Spoiled Children." At Christmas, her classmates went skiing in Gstaad or to Maui with their dads' agents. Everyone's dad was in the movie biz. She may never have gone on a real trip with her family, and now I imagined her vacations consisted of calling in sick at the Ritz Grill and staying home to read, or listen to Jackson Browne.

Growing up, I loved Jackson Browne too, but for me, Joni Mitchell was the truer muse: her plangent voice; her sense of otherness. "Life is for learning," she assured me, and I wanted to believe her.

I want my daughters to believe that, too.

College was a new start for me, as I imagine it was for Lacey, but fear strafed every landscape, giving each the same striations, like a strobe. Joe was left behind in Lloyd Harbor, but everything about our bruising romance had accompanied me to New Haven, even as I spent dutiful hours in the library, where striving gave the study carrels a neon buzz.

Then around 11:00 PM, I would put on tight leather pants and a cropped top and go out, picking up an engineering graduate student at a party one night, an actor at the Yale School of Drama the next.

The actor was particularly kind. When I awoke beside him the next morning, I asked if we had "done it."

"If we do, you'll know," he said gently.

I didn't know how I would know.

I was so cut off from my physicality, even as I tussled with boys in the backs of trucks, grinding beneath them on park benches in the sad city green. Often I would find myself in the rooms of guys named Scott or Keith, who played ice hockey and majored in poli-sci, who could be counted on not to understand. We would tremble on their beds, but at some point, I would begin to scream, and they would recoil. Before I knew it, I was running—flushed, half-naked—into the New Haven night.

Was this normal?

These were nice boys, but I forced them to hurt me, not to pleasure me, tempting them to kiss me. Kiss me *hard*. Take me into the alley behind Rudy's Bar, slam me against the wall, bite my neck, my shoulder, shove your hand down my skirt. I was rough with them, too, playful, taunting, challenging. The alley, cut through with the smell of vomit, was the right place for us to find each other, feel each other, helped by drink and the late, late hour and the cold. My friend Judy's Siberian husky would put his paw in his water dish when he was drinking, to evoke the memory of snow. He liked the cold, missed it. I wondered if I did, too; if I missed the drama with Joe. I would recruit these boys to the alley, as the night swelled around us like a tsunami, to writhe beneath them on broken glass.

Technically, I was still a virgin, but I felt anything but inexperienced. I felt soiled, used up, undeserving of the tentative gesture or the polite glance. That's why I was so taunting, so teasing, daring these nice boys to seem violent, even in their Brooks Brothers sweaters. They might comply, but they were always shamefaced afterward.

Still, I worked hard, spending hours in the Cross Campus Library, watching as couples lolled on the grass in the early, unexpected days of spring.

They seemed blurry in their innocence, while I felt broken, as uneasy in the brocaded world of the academy as in the alley with splintered glass.

In December of my junior year, Joe left a phone message: "Can I see you?" I agreed to meet him at Rockefeller Center, near the Christmas tree. There he was, looking simultaneously dapper and foolish, and I remembered how handsome he was. He lurched forward—to kiss me?—and I jerked away, and he laughed that goofy laugh, so high for a man so menacing.

"How you doing?" His voice was gruff.

"I'm okay. How are you?"

"I'm great." He smiled at me.

I wanted to say, "You look great," but what I really wanted to say was "I hate you. You ruined my life. You *almost* ruined my life."

"I'm happy to see you," he said. "I never thought I would."

"Be happy to see me?"

He looked at me sideways and laughed. "No. See you again."

We fell into an uncomfortable silence, leaning against the railing, watching figures etch the ice with all the grace our dancing together had always lacked. The skaters seemed carefree, harmonious, the kind of "vivid and responsive peace" Wallace Stevens wrote about. Joe always hated "literary shit" like that. He never wanted to know what I was reading or thinking, and we didn't share jokes or insights. We had no friends in common, no movies we both loved. Yet I was bound to him, and I remembered wondering: How will we ever disconnect?

At the time I thought we might never disconnect.

"Can I buy you a coffee?" he asked to break the silence, reaching into his battered leather coat for his wallet.

Suddenly, I was afraid to leave the protective crush of the crowd. Flocks of children in their warm coats. Sunlight glinting off the Christmas ornaments. There was a kind of safety in that. "How about here?" I gestured at a trolley dispensing cappuccino. I ordered a tea, struggling with the tea bag, with the too-hot cup, needing another cup to contain the heat.

"Thanks."

"No worries," he said, reaching over to touch my arm, friendly not flirtatious, and I spilled my tea, watching it trickle down the front of my coat. I hadn't worn my "good" coat in case something happened. What did I expect to happen? What was I even doing here?

It had always been like this: my brain moving too fast, darting nervously, dodging the intimacy, not knowing how to control his power over me. For I had *drawn* him to me then, hadn't I, just as I had today? And for what? Did I want him to be dangerous, to break open all the things that even then I found stifling about my life? Even at sixteen, didn't I want him to be rough, not to hurt me, but to challenge me, to disorient me from homework and college, my parents' plans?

"I heard you still wanna be a writer," Joe said. "That's cool."

"You're a trainer, right?"

"Yeah. Most of the time. I'm married. My wife's father owns a pharmacy. Sometimes I work there. But we don't really get along." He winked and laughed. "Maybe he doesn't trust me with the meds."

"You're *married?*"

"Crazy, huh? I know." He took a sip of his coffee. "And I've got a kid."

"You do?"

"It's hers. From somebody else. They were never married. Will. He's big. He's like eleven now."

"Wow."

"Yeah. It's been tough. For him, I mean, more than me."

"Why?"

"Well, you know. What happened with you? That's been happening with him."

"IT HAS?"

"Yeah. Not the sex part. I'm no fucking pervert. But you know. The hitting."

The *hitting?* I was too stunned to speak.

"I hate myself for it. I do. I know you won't believe that."

You don't know me at all, I wanted to say.

He lowered his voice. "Shit. I even tried to kill myself. Pills, you know. From the old man's pharmacy. No wonder he won't let me work there, right?"

He winced, and I couldn't tell if the sunlight was making him sensitive. I remembered a different sun, the day he took me rowing in the harbor in a stolen rowboat, Jenny the dog balancing nervously on the bow. I remembered Joe smoking a joint, the Bee Gees blaring, as the wind kicked up and Jenny shivered. I remembered a sky growing sullen with the promise of rain. Across the water, I could see my parents' house, the one my mother had designed, nestled among oak trees, looking storybook safe. But I wasn't safe there, and I was the only one who knew it. I had never been safe.

Why do you do it, Joe, I wanted to shout, *to that child, to me, to all the others? Why did you twist us away from happiness? Why was it a secret? Why so brutal, so constant, or did I seek you out? Did you do it because I wanted you to?*

"Is he okay, that boy?" I asked quietly, not wanting to rile Joe, even as I clutched the cup of tea, knowing I would never drink it now.

He shrugged. "He'll be fine. Look, my dad used to beat the shit outta me. I got over it. Like you did."

I thought: *You* really *don't know me at all.*

And maybe I didn't really know myself any better than I ever had. What was I doing here? I should have been in New Haven studying. Working on a drawing for Vincent Scully's class on art and architecture. I had been lucky to get in, but the assignments were hard. They involved drawing. Being able to see without the scrim, the veil, that cleaved me from life.

I was here because I needed to know . . . what? If he had loved me? If he felt bad? If he ever regretted what he did? If he ever told anyone? If he tried to stop? If he was still dancing? If he was the reason I never danced again?

"Why did you do it?" I blurted out, unaware even that I was going to say it.

He drew a long, troubled breath and mumbled something I could hardly hear. "Because."

"*Because?*"

He shrugged.

"I knew you were too young, but I wanted to have you. Before anyone else did."

But that wasn't the reason. *There was no reason.* The brutality had an almost slapstick quality, it was so unpremeditated.

"And what about your stepson? What's his name? Will? What's going to happen to him?"

He gulped down the last of his coffee. "He'll get over it," he repeated. "Like you did."

And before I knew it, he was gone.

The summer before my senior year, I tried to shore up my credentials by working as a speechwriter for a political consultant named David Garth. Garth's specialty was the hard-hitting television ad, with a barrage of facts superimposed over the candidate's face.

My supervisor, Saul, became a close friend: I thought I had found that elusive solidarity, that sense of refuge, I had been seeking for so long. Saul had also gone to Yale and then to England to study literature, which I dearly wanted to do. He had written a book with Ram Dass, a compendium of services for the needy called *May I Help You?*, but the typesetter had screwed up the title and an early galley read *May I Hlep You?* "Hlep" became our code word for the moments when our co-workers, all avid politicos, seemed oblivious or too aggressive. Those were the moments we closed Saul's office door, so we could talk freely about books and babies: His wife, Astrid, was hugely pregnant and spending the summer at a friend's farm. They had lost an earlier baby, and Astrid thought the lazy rhythm of rural life would make this pregnancy more peaceful. The baby who died was named Jessica. So Saul called me "Jessifer" instead.

In the long summer afternoons, I would entertain him with stories of my addled romantic adventures. The other men in the office were nerds, sweaty and earnest and overweight. So I had resorted to my shadow life, meeting men on the steps of the Metropolitan Museum, and going home with them, and (almost) having sex. Mostly they were nice boys from Ivy League schools who had summer jobs that they, too, would have to make seem more interesting on paper.

Then one day, crossing Fifth Avenue at 57th Street, an older man with slicked back hair smiled at me, and I smiled back. We were walking in opposite directions, but he bounded back toward me to catch my arm. We began to talk and he invited me back to his apartment and we smoked a joint together. Later, I learned it had been laced with PCP.

I didn't reappear at the office for two days. I don't even know how I got home. I vaguely remember stumbling onto a bus. I don't remember unlocking the door of the apartment on Bank Street, where the two girls with whom I was renting rarely slept. Two days, and no one said a word, not the sweaty politicos, jockeying for leverage with the candidates. I wouldn't have expected them to notice. But what about Saul? He had lost one Jessica, and now he had almost lost another.

But Saul, the man with whom I thought I'd finally found a connection, never called, never reached out. How was that possible?

I had loved Saul and trusted him. We had so much in common. I had listened to his dreams for his daughter, his longing for his wife. But I couldn't count on him to look out for me, to wonder about my whereabouts.

He hadn't even noticed I was gone.

I suspected that Lacey had a different sense of otherness. It tailed her from her days of waitressing at the Ritz Grill. But she rocketed ahead, never slowing down, finishing her degree in three years, hurtling forward. She was as active as I was fixed. Yet we were looking for the same thing, a sense of clarity, stability. *Normalcy.* And we thought the Rhodes, with its lustre and deep pockets, might provide or certify it.

After I won the Scholarship, I called Saul to tell him and thank him for his reference letter. We would have more in common now, not just Yale, but England, too. And the daughter named Jessica, whose loss had created another kind of bond between us; we never spoke of her spectral presence. Juliet, his new baby, was due any day. The weeks after I won were strange; when I went on a holiday with my family, I could sense my brothers' hostility. *They* were special, the ones who should be taking up space. They had verve, or spark, or whatever the Rhodes people were seeking. I know now they just wanted someone to see them, too.

Before the Christmas break, the *Yale Daily News* sent a student to photograph me. In no other photo do I look less like myself. I wore the same ensemble I had confected for the interviews, complete with faux pearls and sensible pumps. My smile seems uncertain—I have never liked having my photo taken, anyway—as if they could rescind the Rhodes at any time. Others looked like they were posing for a stamp, but I was reprising an earlier performance, the person I had been in the interviews. The person Saul thought he was mentoring: hopeful, purposeful. *Normal.*

That impersonation, hastily improvised, had worked, at least for a while.

Then, the following fall, I found someone with whom I really could be myself. He practically landed at my feet. Accidentally: he tumbled down the stairs at a party and lay on the hardwood floor, soused and smiling, his hand placed ceremoniously in the pocket of his good wool coat.

"Don't move him," I urged, ever the doctor's daughter. "He may have broken something."

"Nah," his friend muttered. "He never breaks anything but hearts."

Days later, walking down Elm Street, the heartbreaker hollered from the sidewalk, "Whatcha gonna be for Halloween?"

I smiled shyly. Did he remember me?

"I'm going to be green," he said, making his way to Rudy's Bar.

"Last time I saw you, you were green," I told him, and he grinned.

That was the moment he was caught, and I was caught, as I had never been since Joe. I was dazzled by his ease, his intelligence, his cramped handwriting. His limp: he had been hit—purposely, an eyewitness said—by a drunk driver as he weaved home through the streets of New Haven on his bike. The metal plate in his leg had disabled his athletic dreams, but he went on writing poems, the little "I do this, I do that" poems Frank O'Hara favored, as if he had embraced O'Hara's affirmation:

> *in a sense we're all winning*
> *we're alive*

Nicholas was my first real love, and when we made love for the first time—it was my first time ever—I asked him why he had never pushed me, the only man who never had.

"I wanted to wait until you were ready," he said tenderly.

I pierced my ears a week later to mark that moment, and he held my hand.

With Nick, I had that feeling that only the besotted know: a romantic complicity that felt inclusive, never extreme. There was so much love and understanding and excitement, it spilled beyond the immediate bounds of our bodies, cascading over walls into flowerbeds, nourishing plants. I felt something else, too, that I had never felt before: a wholeness, completeness, more rapturous than any sorcerer's spell. At night, when he lay beside me in my little bed, contentment cloaked me like a blanket. The dampening shame inside me seemed to grow quiet as well.

I didn't know contentment had such quietude and, perversely, I wanted everyone else to know as well. Nick was so genial, so graceful, so beloved. How had he ended up with *me?* Once, when we were awakened by a fire alarm, he told me he would dress quickly and slip out the back gate. But I wouldn't let him. I wanted him to join the other students spilling into the courtyard, dazed and disheveled, in their slippers and robes.

"They're going to take some kind of roll call," he protested. "It'll be awkward. This isn't my college."

"No one minds. Besides, it's not a real fire drill. It's just a bunch of people in their pajamas, looking annoyed."

"It's a test." He smiled. "And I hate tests. You know that."

"But if it's real and you perish in the flames, I'll never forgive myself."

"I won't be too happy either," he said, following me down the stairs. I knew there was no fire. But I also knew everyone would notice him, looking sheepish and irresistible. I just wanted to show him off.

Even to my mother, who drove up to New Haven to meet him later that month, gliding up in her Subaru as I waited on the street.

"At the corner, we'll make a left on Elm," I said when I got in, even though I was a terrible navigator.

We stopped in front of Rudy's Bar, and my mother leaned over, peering out the window on my side.

"He hangs out here?"

"Sometimes. Well, a lot."

"On a Tuesday, in the afternoon?"

"He doesn't have class in the afternoon on Tuesdays."

"Daddy told me he's an ambassador's son. I hear his parents have a place on the Vineyard."

"Nantucket."

"That sounds nice."

Yes, he was an ambassador's son. But he was also an alcoholic. No one seemed to acknowledge that. At first, I didn't realize it, either. The sweet, slightly rancid taste of his mouth didn't alarm me. How could I find fault with him, when he was so strong and funny and charming? He loved literature. And he loved me.

After months of dating, Nick took me to his parents' summer home on Nantucket. The ferry from Woods Hole made a winter crossing only twice a day. We were almost alone on deck, wind tearing at our cheeks, eyes streaming, as the boat forged through the frigid waters. I had never been happier.

But when I went back to his parents' home, months later, to

spend a weekend with them, things were icy in a different way. His mother was a glamorous, highly prickly Washington doyenne. His father was, well, an ambassador. His twin brother was there, but he seemed to spend most of his time stalking a famous singer who had a cottage farther down the beach. She was much older, but she seemed to like him, and he was thrilled. I don't think he'd ever had a serious girlfriend. We had that in common, that awkwardness, the opposite of the grace, the fluidity, of his brother. So we would eye each other warily.

Late one afternoon, after a game of tennis, as his mother was preparing her second gin and tonic, I told her softly, "I think Nick's an alcoholic."

"Excuse me?"

"Nick drinks. A lot. In the middle of the day. Most days."

"I don't know what you're talking about."

"I'm worried. He drinks, and then he drives."

"Nicky? No, he's very careful. He was hit by a drunk driver, for God's sake."

"Yes, and I think his leg still hurts. I think he should see someone about it."

"You have a lot of ideas about him, don't you?"

I was silent.

"Your father's a doctor, right?"

My father had really taken to Nick, even taken him to the tennis matches at Forest Hills. He liked that Nick didn't order the most expensive sandwich, the lobster club. My father wanted to refer Nick to a new orthopedist to examine the plate in his leg—an unusual amount of interest for my father to show in anyone else. But he liked that Nick was an ambassador's son.

So I said, yes, my father was a cardiologist. He didn't work on bones. But he thought the fact that Nick's leg still hurt so much, after more than two years, wasn't a good sign.

"That's why he's drinking," I said. "I think. His leg hurts."

"He's got to be patient and let it heal."

"But meanwhile, he's missing classes. I'm really worried about him."

"Does he know you're telling his mother all this?"

In that moment, I realized I'd collided with the code of WASP privilege I had grown up with but never understood: the mother, at a slumber party, who made breakfast for all the girls but didn't offer me bacon, since I was Jewish and "couldn't eat it." (My family did.) The birthday celebrations at the Winter Club with skates and mufflers and hot chocolate—everything but Jews, who couldn't be members then. Here, in the world of custom saddles and cotillion classes, there was always a sense of what one could and could not say. But I only knew I had strayed when I tripped over the boundary. God knows, I was good at tripping over things. I wasn't as good at understanding the nuances of power and privilege. The people Nick's parents played doubles with, they were Jewish, weren't they? I guess one could have Jewish friends across the net, but only because the patriarch was a powerful Washington lawyer.

A Jewish girlfriend was probably pushing it.

"I really love him. I want to help him," I said, more quietly now.

"And I'm sure he cares about you. As for the drinking . . . " She leaned in, narrowing her pewter-colored eyes. "I don't think you know much about drinking. Your people don't drink."

My *people?* I didn't *have* any people. Nick was all I had. But his parents were as clueless, differently clueless, as mine: they, too, weren't looking, or didn't want to see.

In Nantucket, I got to know Nick's brothers and sisters, but there was another brother who'd been lost years ago, before Nick and his twin were even conceived. He drowned in the waters off Cape Cod one summer, when he was just a toddler. His father discovered his tiny body in the water, stubbing his toe against the corpse.

Nick never spoke of the brother he lost, yet he never lived far from his shadow, even when he moved to London my second year at Oxford, taking a flat in Bayswater. We spent our weekends there, huddled against the strangeness of our situation, the things we could not say: that he, too, was drowning. He was drinking himself to death.

I tried to help Nick, but really I could not fix him, I was so broken myself. Love doesn't salve, doesn't save, no one can be rescued, tiny body beneath the waves. Lacey had a man she loved, who loved her. It wasn't enough.

I never told Nick I was applying for a Rhodes. I didn't want him to think I was running away. He seemed happy that I won, but mostly he seemed dazed. He spent more time at Rudy's after that. When he deposited me on the pier in New York for the embarkment, the forklift operator pointed to his tiny orange Honda: "Is that going, too?"

Nick laughed, but I could feel my sadness swelling. I couldn't believe I was leaving him, everything he had given me, behind.

Was I running away? Again? Maybe. But I felt I was running *toward*. My escape to Paris had been brief, but the Rhodes would allow a longer, more leisurely respite. And maybe I would finally be securing my future, not just fleeing my past.

18.

To my surprise, Oxford looked a lot like Yale, only the glorious towers were legitimately gothic. I loved the winding cobble-stoned lanes, students rattling past on rusted bikes. I lived in the Daubeny Building, a former laboratory at the head of the Botanic Garden, and though I didn't have a view, I had something even more highly prized: a private shower stall. That saved me, with my phobias, from having to use the communal tub.

Even before the QE2 docked, many of us felt "gob-smacked"—there is no equivalent word in American English—as if we had barrelled through the looking glass. (No matter, Lewis Carroll, Alice's creator, was himself an Oxford don.) The porter on the ship swore to "knock us up" in the morning (meaning he would wake us at a designated hour) and an elegant passenger leaned over to inquire of the man beside her, "May I pinch your nuts?" (referring to the bowl of cashews beside his Merlot). At Christ Church, one of the most elite Oxford colleges, a waiter once chided me when I dawdled over my dinner. "Don't make a meal of it!" he scolded. (I thought it *was* a meal.) Another woman remembered using the wrong bit of cutlery, scraping it extremely noisily, then picking it up and licking it. "At least in this one area, I was the equal of any male Rhodes scholar," she laughed.

But there were moments of elegance no Yankee could spoil: fancy dress parties at private estates, preceded by luncheon in the formal gardens, where the conifers dated from the seventeenth century. Or tea in the library, all carved wood and cracked leather, graced by the occasional Holbein or an equestrian portrait by George Stubbs. When we ascended to our bedrooms, their large sash windows overlooking the parkland, we would find our dresses laid out on the bed. Women were expected to have a "lie-down" before the dancing commenced, and it was one form of chauvinism to which I never objected. (I never declined an opportunity to nap.)

Magdalen, the college where I lived, had admitted women only two years before my arrival, having been robustly male for more than five centuries. Women could dine with Oxford dons, but it meant ascending a precarious staircase in the near dark, then sidling along the wall to find our places. "High table"—as it was called—was almost inaccessible to high heels. It's no wonder some women lost their footing: we seemed as exotic as the collection of human oddities in the Ashmolean Museum. Exotic and abashed: When I told one tutor I was "at Magdalen," he thought I said I was "modeling."

Some of the most confident Rhodes women felt derailed, wondering what had become of their contacts and competitive instincts, unsure how to plug in the teakettle or coax the little wall heater with coins. It was not uncommon to struggle with what one female scholar called "feelings of inadequacy; the sense that we had to *perform* our excellence in order to prove (to whom? Ourselves?) that we deserved to be there; the confusion at how to reconcile our personal lives with the exciting, terrifying injunction to 'fight the world's fight.'"

Women at Oxford had long been an object of speculation, even derision. As Christopher Hobhouse wrote in 1939:

Relatively few men go to lectures, the usefulness of which was superseded some while ago with the invention of the printing press. The women, docile and literal, continue to flock to every lecture with medieval zeal, and record in an hour of longhand scribbling what could have been assimilated in ten minutes in an armchair.

In truth, the British regarded Rhodes scholars of either sex with equal skepticism, echoing the character in Max Beerbohm's novel *Zuleika Dobson:*

Americans have a perfect right to exist. But he did often find himself wishing Mr. Rhodes had not enabled them to exercise that right in Oxford.

Still, the history of outliers at Oxford was unusually distinguished, including everyone from Oscar Wilde to Evelyn Waugh (whose *Brideshead Revisited* was the *Downton Abbey* of its day). As John Mortimer wrote, "We were middle class boy[s], born to hard professional work, educated above our stations slightly, falling half in love, at Oxford, with a more effete and useless way of life."

Liam Brennan was another of these men, for whom Oxford was more exodus than idyll. John Mortimer's description fit him like a suit from Savile Row. The most gorgeous and canny of the Magdalen College boys, Liam had gone to Princeton but chose to study medicine at Oxford, because the program was so inexpensive compared to the States. Liam had grown up in Ohio with an abusive father, and he arrived in England with little more than his green loden coat. But he spoke several languages, largely self-taught, and he also managed to know everything about Beethoven's late quartets and Hegel's dialectic. He introduced me to mozartkugel, the tiny candies that sweetened the long afternoons.

While Nick stayed at Yale to finish his degree—he would move to London the following autumn—Liam and I gravitated toward each other warily. We were two loners—even, perhaps, two misanthropes—flirting roughly, teasing each other, trying to throw each other off guard. I had never listened to *Parsifal;* I had never been to the Uffizi; I knew nothing about goat cheeses from Tuscany or the best lager to order on tap. Liam did, and he wasn't shy about letting people know, and that, too, annoyed me. But I couldn't wait to catch sight of him, striding down the High Street in his doctor's scrubs.

One day I emerged from class to find him leaning against his bicycle, smoking, and we walked back to Magdalen College in the dusk. When we passed the Wyckham tea room, he rested his bike against the stone wall, and I could smell him—the smell of the cigarettes he rolled himself, cigarettes that would kill him at age fifty-two.

Suddenly he lifted me off the ground, our image reflected in the window of the Wyckham. Joe had lifted me this way, wrenching me out of the world I knew. But in Liam's arms, I felt lighter, almost languorous. It was a relief to be touched, to be lifted, this way. Then he kissed me, a deep kiss that belied all the months of jostling between us; that promised other long walks; long kisses, leaning against the stone.

There were no cell phones in those days; no phones in the rooms at all. (No computers either; they didn't exist.) So Liam began sending me letters every day, volumes of besotted prose, the envelopes crowding my mailbox, pages and pages written in his elegant hand. Our actual romance was halting and fraught, unstable: screaming matches on train platforms and shattered sunglasses and long, sulky silences in the Middle Common Room.

But no one has ever written so beautifully to me:

Jessica, mio Tesoro,

Since writing you the first letter this evening I've been out walking around, and I feel inspired to desecrate yet another blank page. Just wanted to tell you that I caught another whiff of autumn in the air tonight. Miraculous air! No other time of year is so redolent of past times, past selves. It is a cool, voiceless air that hardens glass-like, clarifying and sharpening; it is a vagrant presence that appears one day without warning, transforming all, honing each shaft of light. This strange air which seems to arise by alchemy as summer leaves are fired by the waning sun, vaporized, this vagrant air settles for a time, but is destined soon to move south, again unannounced, and leaves behind the earth strewn with bright, brittle shards. Do you know this air, my Jesling? Do you know that first peculiar autumn smell, a mahogany-colored scent?

His letters were addressed to "carissima" or "mia cara," written on exquisite paper with a calligraphy pen. Sometimes he would give me advice (particularly on how to get rid of Nick); more often he would profess his love for me.

Carissima,

I think of you constantly. Constantly. I can't even look at the college buildings, the streets we've walked along, can't go into a restaurant, get onto my bicycle, pause to sniff a flower, gaze at the night sky, play any piece of music, go to sleep or awaken without thinking of you, my Jesling. It's a constant source of unremitting agony, and yet I'm not really even sure that I want it to end, for it's always mingled with memories that are comforting, pleasurable, hopeful, tender, loving, simply because they are memories of you.

    I mustn't go on like this, though.

    In fact, I can't go on like this. Please forgive me for cutting this short. I hope this finds you well, sweetheart. I love you, Jess. Take care, please. I love you. I do love you, Jess.

Your Liam

At Yale, Nick would leave me furtive notes, scrawled on the back of moving violations from the City of New Haven: "There are flowers in your sink. Apologies." But Liam's letters were overwhelming in their bulk, their relentlessness. There was something indulgent, self-intoxicated, about all those words. And they seemed oblivious to what was really happening between us, for I belonged, still, to Nicholas, to the tenderness of our time together. Every time Liam kissed me, I was betraying Nick.

More and more, the guilt tore at me like the abrading fingers of the cold. I had drawn these two men to me. Did I love either of them? Did I love them both? Nick was moving to England to join me. Liam was talking about marriage. The days grew shorter, more suffocating.

Then I got sick.

Stumbling over the cobblestones in the courtyard of New College, I steeled myself to the cold, and to the wrath of my tutor, who taught the plays of Ben Jonson while sprawled, diva-like, on her leopard-skin rug.

I hadn't done the work.

I was having trouble holding a pencil.

I was having trouble seeing, too.

In the days that followed, the weakness in my right leg got worse, and it wasn't my usual clumsiness. Something was happening, causing my toes to tingle and making my calf numb. I didn't know what it was, but I didn't tell anyone, not even the nice woman who lived next door, training as a doctor, who had also been chosen that icy day in Boston at the regional Rhodes interviews.

I began struggling to form words, my tongue frozen, as if stung by a very cold Popsicle. Like many children of doctors, I tried to diagnose myself. Maybe it was the cold, or the distance from home, or maybe what I'd always feared was finally happening: maybe I was losing my mind.

I took the train to the Queen Square Neurological Hospital in London to see if they could help me, since my brother Douglas was there on a medical rotation from the States. They hospitalized me immediately in a ward for "neurological unknowns." Some patients were in their early twenties; some were already in wheelchairs, including a woman who had just had a baby, a baby we never saw. Late at night, a girl with Tourette's syndrome would shout wild obscenities into the darkened ward. The doctors prodded me with nails and needles, implements that looked like medieval instruments of torture.

They thought I might have multiple sclerosis, a potentially debilitating disease of the central nervous system.

I called my father, but it was my mother who came, erecting her seawall of books in a little Quaker bed and breakfast. Sitting beside me in the ward, day after day, listening to the cries of the other women, she bent over her newspaper or her needlepoint. I would lie in bed, defiantly wearing eyeliner and black punk boots with my sea-green hospital gown. When the doctors made rounds, my mother looked away—out of modesty, perhaps—or because she avoided bad news with the delicacy, finality, of a cat.

One afternoon when she was sitting with me in the hospital— she said she knew I was going to be okay because I was wearing eyeliner—Liam strode toward us, glorious in his loden coat.

"He's wonderful," my mom murmured under her breath.

"I know," I whispered back. "But so is Nicholas."

"It won't be either of them," she said, with characteristic certainty.

That was comforting, but I wanted to know more about making these choices, about the way life unspools, just as Isabel does now. I was waiting, in my hospital gown, to re-enter the world, to return to Oxford. I wasn't sure I could live on my own again. I needed her to say more, and maybe her feelings would show themselves like flowers, in all their rapturous color, their lavish charm. Maybe she would say, "I believe in you," and we could finally talk— not just about Liam and Nicholas and Ben Jonson. But about Joe.

Several weeks later, we returned to Magdalen, my diagnosis still uncertain. She walked with me, slowly, around the walled garden; a garden that was gorgeous and multilayered, centuries old. It was still cold and not much was growing, but she showed me where things would sprout up in a matter of months, if I could wait. I wanted to believe in the virtues of patience, of forbearance, but what I really wanted was to be embraced. I needed my mother, the architect, to bridge the gulf between us. She was an expert navigator. Maybe she could re-orient me? But that day, in the frigid garden, pointing out where plants would one day thrive, she offered all the warmth she could, all the intimacy.

The next day, she flew back to New York.

I returned to my room at Magdalen, where Daniel, who lived next door, had placed daisies in the doorway in a broken pot. He and I began watching late-night reruns of *The Mary Tyler Moore Show* on the blinking telly in the Middle Common Room, eating Indian takeout on the filthy floor. Soon we were joined by other graduate students—graduate students were, by definition, outsiders—all of whom were foreigners, struggling to pay their bursar's bills and finish their degrees.

It felt good to have people to talk to, about the tutor who fell asleep mid-session, while his student watched a spindle of drool trace its way from his mouth to his knee, like a spidery suspension bridge. About the committee that became fixated on the color, rather than the content, of someone's thesis, wondering if the pages were ecru or buff or cream. "You'll have to use cream-out on your mistakes!" the committee members chortled. These stories never failed to amuse us. We were far from home, and contact with our families was sporadic, attenuated (this was in the days when very few public phones—and there *were* public phones—allowed international calls). You could trudge down to the "towne centre," a twenty-minute trek, and plunge your coins into the phone for a call that would leave you more disoriented than comforted. Or you could head to the Middle Common Room for some Guinness and Mary Tyler Moore.

Something still lingers from the moment, more than the numbness in the ring finger on my right hand. It is the salvation we find in the presence of others, in the warm pitch of someone's laugh. The shared pleasure of midnight dashes across the Deer Park and picnics on the shores of the Cherwell; duck pâté from the covered market and satsumas, if the season allows. Like Lacey, I had been alone, reinventing myself with the desperate ingenuity of the disenfranchised. There had never been a safety net. Now, for the first time, there was quirky Daniel, who could rhyme any word in the English language, even "porringer"; and Patrick, who made exquisite pasta with little more than a can of sardines. And Peggy, whose father was a famous, and famously private, writer. And Jane, who was in love with Daniel, whose parodies of the "goonish quaintisms" of the British delighted us all. Martin dated a flame-haired Australian, a poet, and assured us her hair really was that color. He knew because he'd seen her without clothes. We were oddballs together—family to each other when our own families were broken or far away—with Oscar Wilde, Magdalen's presiding spirit, as our patron saint.

For the first time I felt part of something bigger, if only fleetingly.

And I had to believe that, during her Oxford days, Lacey also felt sated: that her hunger to belong had finally been eased. Maybe she had even confided her fears to someone. Did I ever tell Patrick, over sardine-infused pasta, what was troubling me?

Daniel and I talked about everything from Molière to Margaret Thatcher. Did I ever tell him about Joe?

Perhaps no one ever knows how much pain someone else is in. Even if they tell us, it's impossible to hear. We can't put gas in the car or plan a menu or purchase cotton balls if we know how harsh and broken, how ruined, the lives around us are. Meanwhile, we are making a mess of the lives we have—gifted, sunlit, filled with spouses who smell good, who like to laugh. I didn't want to make a mess of my life anymore. JESSIAC it said on the bracelet Isabel created for me, back when she was Dolores. I always thought it might have said MANIAC instead. I *would* be a maniac if I failed to value, to protect, this peaceful, pleasant world I'd been lucky enough to land in. If I let Joe's savagery reach across decades to destroy this, too.

19.

Kyle had spoken of Lacey's death as "the catalyst that destroyed my family," adding, "I'm very protective of the family I have left."

No one was left of his original family, other than his sister, Corinne. His mother had seen to that by, as Kyle put it, "duplicating Lacey's feat."

I didn't want to ask about his mother's suicide. Even in this conversation—so raw, so revealing—it felt too fraught. But Kyle went on, as if in answer to my thoughts: "My mother became consumed by Lacey's death." He said it without compassion or remorse. "My mom just poured attention into Lacey. There was a lot of pressure to be her shining star. Lacey hated it."

"Did Lacey ever talk to your mother about it?"

"My mother wouldn't have been receptive. Corinne was probably the most passionate of all of us. She was wild. She was not successful in ways that would make my mother proud. My dad always had a special relationship with Corinne. He understood her; they were black sheep together."

"And you?"

"I was the youngest, spoiled by my mother. Lacey felt she had a duty to protect me. She felt she had to help me be well-rounded, balanced, to instill liberal values."

I wanted to ask what "liberal values" meant. The phrase felt condensed, like those soups that are supposed to be healthy, but with ingredients too segregated, too desiccated, to do good. Instead, I asked him about his childhood.

"I came from a broken home. My parents divorced very early."

"And you lived with your mother and stepfather?"

"Yeah. Robert. He was a prick. Robert was incredibly jealous of my mother's relationship with her kids, especially Lacey."

"Why Lacey most of all?"

"She publicly adored Lacey. Lacey's accomplishments defined my mother in a public sense. It drove my stepdad nuts. He felt her relationship with her kids was the most important thing to her.

"My mother became as completely enveloped in Lacey's death as she had been in her life," Kyle said. "Grief, self-pity consumed her, defined her. She would work into conversation with complete strangers that her daughter killed herself. You know, at some point, people don't want to talk about it anymore. They want to let the grieving process take its course."

He was silent for a moment.

"She went to the same hotel. The same room. We found out later that she had been there for a few days. Lacey left a suicide note filled with apologies: 'I love you, Simon. I love you, Kyle. I can't face the horrors.' My mom's note was all about Lacey. She left an audiocassette tape; I've never listened to it. Corinne has."

I hadn't known his mother left an audiotape.

"Having to tell Simon about Lacey was the hardest thing I've ever done. I can still hear him wail in that airport. My dad was the third casualty. He died of a heart attack. He was so incredibly emotionally invested in Lacey. My family's story is like a Greek tragedy. Absurd."

I mentioned Lacey's car crash. Kyle said it had happened the week before her death. At the time, he'd wondered if "there was trauma from the accident that put her in a depressive downward spiral."

"Ten days before she died," he went on, "there was a knock on my window at 3:00 AM. Lacey was there, all disheveled, looking like crap, her face cut, dazed. I carried her to my car. She said she couldn't sleep, so she went driving on Mulholland and she veered off down into a gorge. She climbed out and was picked up by a police cruiser and dropped off in front of my house. She had a broken tooth, so I took her to the ER. The next day she was released from the hospital, and we went up to Mulholland to find the car.

"But we couldn't find it. Finally, the police flew a helicopter over and saw it. It was 100 yards down the gorge. The car was completely destroyed. The air bag had deployed. She had climbed her way out of the gorge, and when the police saw her, they accused her of being on drugs. She had a concussion and she was bleeding, but they dropped her off at my house."

"What did she say?"

"She was concerned about Chatsworth, how they'd be upset if she didn't go to work the next day. I was thrilled she was alive. I remember telling Simon she was fine."

I wondered if he regretted telling Simon that.

Lacey checked into the Century Park Hotel in Century City and called from a pay phone to say she was taking time off. She assured him that Chatsworth was being understanding. And she said she loved him. "She thanked me for everything I'd done.

"She felt like she was a burden on me, on our family, on everyone. You know, when people talk about it, about suicide, they *mean* it. You need to thank God, or Allah, that you can get in there and help them."

If *you can get in there and help,* I thought.

20.

After two years in England, I couldn't wait to leave. I wanted to hold a real job, with deadlines and coffee breaks. I was ready to say good-bye to my friends and tutors, to the glorious Botanic Gardens, even to my private shower stall. The last weeks were a whirlwind: my thesis on Shakespeare was accepted; I "sat" my exams, in full robes and mortarboard; and when I received my degree, I processed through the splendid Sheldonian Theatre, dazzled by the pageantry and dazed from lack of sleep. My friends greeted me afterward with strawberries and champagne, and we spent the summer together—Daniel and Patrick and Jane and Martin—knowing it was idyllic time we would never have again.

By then, Liam had left for Cambridge to complete his medical studies. We had stopped seeing each other long before Nick moved to London, but sometimes, when I gazed out the window of the Daubeny Building late at night, I could see Liam standing in the distance, looking up at my lighted window.

Nick flew back to New York with the promise that we would reunite when I got there, although we didn't. (By the time I arrived, he had taken up with someone else.) Nick was headed to graduate school, but I didn't know where *I* was headed. What does one *do* with an MPhil degree in Renaissance drama, anyway?

I had no idea. So when my friend Lori's parents offered to find me an internship at the Mark Taper Forum, a prestigious theater in Los Angeles, I was thrilled. Besides, I liked Lori's parents, partly because when we met, they didn't seem to mind that I was wearing my bathrobe and bunny slippers in the hallway in the middle of the day. They accepted my explanation ("I'm studying for exams") without comment and told me someone from the Taper would interview me. That turned out to be Niall, also a Rhodes scholar, who was passing through Oxford on his way to scale the Himalayas. He sat on the floor of my room and regaled me with tales of his fancy, famous L.A. friends. Chattering away like a steroidal bunny, Niall seemed grandiose and self-dramatizing, clown-sized glasses obscuring his red-rimmed eyes.

"He's the biggest phony I've ever met," I told Lori, though I didn't expect her to relay that to her parents. Nor for them to tell him.

They did.

"Hire that girl!" was his response.

So I went to work at the Mark Taper Forum, where I sat in an office inundated with hundreds of scripts, writing letters to playwrights to help them "fix" their plays. I was delighted to have business cards and desk supplies and paychecks, to be thought of as someone who could "fix" something, *anything*. I loved my job: sitting in on rehearsal, taking copious notes about nothing, flirting with the actors who had the fewest lines.

Over ten years, I climbed the literary ladder, from intern to literary manager to dramaturg, as the whirr and bustle of colleagues blew past my door. I commissioned and developed scripts as a kind of literary midwife and helped actors explore classic texts. My boss, Gordon Davidson, could be winning, climbing onstage in his battered sneakers to welcome theater audiences. Although I'll never forget when he hissed, during the premiere of *Ragtime,* "It doesn't work! You can't make a play about revenge!" What about *Macbeth?* I wanted to challenge him. What about *Sweeney Todd?*

I thought about this for days, making mental lists of plays about vengeance. Was there any juicier subject? What did "vengeance" mean? Why did I never seek redress from my parents, who must have known someone was hurting me? Couldn't they see the welts and gashes? Couldn't they hear Joe coming to my room at night? Nor did I seek help from my dance teacher and his wife, who knew Joe had preyed on other dancers. They watched, day after day, as I followed him upstairs to his attic room. I'm sure they could hear the beatings and see the blood, but they never stepped in to stop him. Much later I learned why: Vinnie was in love with him, and wanted to sleep with Joe himself.

At the Taper I learned that stage lighting had three properties: color, direction, and intensity. I loved the feeling of standing onstage in the light. But I remained behind the scenes, whispering in the playwright's ear about a stray line or a tedious monologue, or advising the director on the impact of a scene. Once I urged a playwright to re-imagine his script, about a young girl who was being abused, even writing lines for her character. Even coaching the young actress on how to say them.

But I had no words of my own.

What about *Antigone,* the young woman lost in a swell of tears?

What about *Medea,* the red-hot fury of revenge?

I could coach a young actress, all hair and freckles and attitude, on how to play an abuse survivor, how to show rage and disbelief and terror and sadness and shame.

But I felt no connection to the pain she postured at, night after night, and twice on Saturdays. As always, I was trying *not* to feel.

Over the course of several months, as I mined my experience for them, the playwright and director never asked why I was so familiar with a survivor's demons. Maybe they presumed all women knew what it meant to be afraid. When Joe had been hurting me, I used to wonder if he had beaten other women in the dance company. (I learned much later that he had.) I thought the older dancers were just too discreet, too mature, to mention it. All those years ago, I fiddled with the contents of my dance bag, looking up at them from the steps below, but I never talked to them about it. It never occurred to me to ask. Here was another sisterhood that might have saved me, strengthened me. But I was unable to connect.

That was still true now, all these years later, wasn't it? Married, a mother of two, I had found an elysian happiness, but could not feel its embrace. One day after school, I took Isabel and Charlotte for a snack, and they were getting along fairly well, each eating something healthy; two things of which most mothers dream. I leaned into their faces, so round, so warm, like apples, and thought of how much I cherished them, yet I despaired. If this couldn't make me happy—being with them, loving them—then maybe nothing ever would.

But happiness, like luck, is serendipitous, not to be willed. The more we chase it, the more it cuts and runs. Maybe we can never know why we are chosen, or shoved aside, or beckoned to, as in a dream. I would have to choose love, randomly, like the women rummaging through the pile of t-shirts. I would have to choose hope, as willfully, definitively, as Lacey did not.

"If you don't know where you're going, any road will get you there," Lewis Carroll suggested, with his unique blend of pointedness and inscrutability. I didn't know where I was going. But I knew I would have to be bold.

21.

That meant being willing to cross boundaries—of discretion, decorum—like asking Lacey's brother for a photograph of her. I realized that I had spent hours and hours thinking of her, feeling our kinship. But I had never actually seen her face.

Kyle kindly sent what he called his "favorite" photo of Lacey. Tellingly, it was a picture of *them*. She, with her dark, urgent features, was leaning against the battered red leather of a restaurant banquette, her arm draped around her little brother. He was baring his teeth, looking ferocious, even as she looked bemused. Lacey's head appeared too big for her body, as if placed there by some kind of digital magic, and she seemed far older than her years.

I couldn't imagine what it would be like to feel that closeness. My own brothers were perpetually competing, with each other and with me. Our life together was thwarted and cramped, full of collusions and suppressions, all the tensions born of shared bathrooms and pilfered notebooks and contested sleep.

Later that night, I thanked Kyle for the photo, and he said he was four or five years old when it was taken. Lacey was probably eight. I asked if he would share another photo with me, of Lacey and Simon in Oxford on their wedding day.

He launched immediately into a memory of the festivities, when the wedding party walked down the High Street from the church. "Lacey looked stunningly beautiful, and Simon was handsome in his suit."

"Had you met Simon before?"

"On a few instances. The first time, when Simon went into the next room, I remember turning to my sister and saying, 'I like him. I approve.' 'I'm not looking for your approval,' she shot back. She was very independent. But she fed off him, his success. She wanted him to love where they were. She missed California, missed the sun. The weather in England depressed her."

He paused. "You know, I'm still in touch with Simon. I stayed with him and his new wife and kids a few weeks ago. He's moved on, and I'm happy for him. He was in the air, on the plane . . . "

Here, Kyle cleared his throat, then plunged ahead, as if the memory of Lacey's last day had its own momentum. "I got the call from the coroner's office the morning Simon was coming . . .

"It was July 4th, and my girlfriend and I were getting ready to go to the beach. We were in my apartment. I got this call. There was a clinical voice, 'Are you related to Lacey Cooper? I'm sorry to tell you your sister's deceased.'

"I collapsed on the floor; I couldn't believe it. For some weird reason, I just couldn't hang up the phone. So I ran upstairs to my neighbors'; I'd never met them, and I opened their door and grabbed their phone and dialed my sister's number. I got her voice mail, and I was yelling, 'Pick up the phone! Pick up the phone!'

"The coroner asked me to come down and identify the body. I realized Simon's flight was arriving at 3:20 PM. I went into 'go' mode, drove to the county coroner's office, got her belongings. They gave me her suicide note. I had to get to LAX, knowing he was coming.

"Simon walked out, expecting to see his wife. Instead I was there. He could see it in my eyes. But I wouldn't have wanted anyone to tell him but me."

Kyle said Simon stayed in L.A. for a year to take on the burden of his mother-in-law. When he left, it was bittersweet for Kyle: Simon was one of the last links to Lacey. But, Kyle insisted, "My family felt no obligation that he should grieve for the rest of his life."

Kyle struck me as such an honorable man, thoughtful, chivalrous, considerate of Simon's pain, relieving him of obligation. This was the person Lacey must have known he could become. Did her death somehow release him, help him emerge as the man she always knew he could be?

"I have lived a life in honor of my sister and my family," he told me. "I still go to her grave a couple of times a year. I talk to her. I bring a picture of my daughter. Lacey's buried in Newport. Cremated and buried there. My mother is buried there, too, far enough away from Lacey not to bother her on a daily basis."

Then Kyle let go an almost-laugh, adding: "And there was no conspiracy at Chatsworth."

"Conspiracy?"

"My sister thinks Lacey was murdered."

This was a stunning revelation. Murdered? What did *he* think?

"Look, Lacey left a suicide note addressed only to myself and Simon, which was hard on other members of my family . . . She wrote the note in her own hand. The door was dead bolted, chain locked from the inside. Corinne thinks Chatsworth was involved in something; Lacey got mixed up in something.

"For Corinne, Lacey's death was crushing. Corinne and Lacey were never tremendously close. They had things left unsaid. Lacey worried that she had taken up so much space in Corinne's life. She used to say 'I love Corinne. I wish I had more in common with her.' Lacey felt guilty that our mother shed all this admiration on her. She felt Corinne never got her due."

Kyle told me how to contact Corinne, who had moved to Maine with a "gentleman" named Robert. Kyle and Corinne lived together for a year and a half after Lacey's suicide. Now they never talked about her death.

I could hear him winding down, as if growing tired from this long safari of revelation, resignation, and grief.

"There were a lot of things I didn't know about my sister," Kyle said quietly. "I got to a point where I didn't care anymore why she did it. I just missed her, and she was gone. Personally, that's when I began to heal. Don't say this to Corinne, but I don't think she's gotten to that point yet. That point beyond feeling guilt."

And what did he feel now?

"I feel a stronger connection to my sister in her death than when she was alive."

22.

That's what I couldn't find, all those years ago. Connection. That's what eluded me, long after I moved to L.A. I would tell the story of Joe to potential lovers, like it was an advisory warning, but I never really thought about it. I couldn't: my past was jagged, remembered in pieces, the way we remember the trauma we have suffered, and survived.

I had gone from the medieval city of dreaming spires to a sprawling mecca of artisanal juices; a city with ample opportunities to be wrapped in seaweed or decode one's dreams. My apartment in Los Feliz was a strange haven, where I ate take-out pizza and wept through reruns of *Hannah and Her Sisters*. I used the apartment as a place to shower and sleep, never to entertain.

For years, I continued to challenge men, to ask them to hurt me. It was the only kind of physical pleasure I knew. Often, in moments of intimacy, I had what one boyfriend, a medical student, called "abreactions," a neurological consequence of being battered. On the cusp of orgasm, I would find myself shaking uncontrollably, or run, screaming, from the room.

More often, I learned not to trap myself in these situations. Besides, I didn't want to sleep with most of these men. I wanted them to want me, and we would grapple in the backs of cars, hurling ourselves at each other, until that fateful moment when I pulled away. Now I can see that what I wanted most was to control them: to punish them for Joe's brutality. But in all other ways I tried to seem charming and accessible, desirable. I pretended I was fine.

One day, a tiny pink message slip appeared in my mailbox at the Taper, with a local phone number. When I called, a woman named Yolanda said she needed to see me right away. I went, as if sleepwalking, to the Women's Crisis Center at Cedars-Sinai Hospital. Yolanda, a heavyset Latina with a kind, used face, ushered me into her office and shut the door.

"I want to talk with you about what happened when you were younger."

I said nothing.

"I'm told you were abused."

"Who told you that?"

"I can't say. But I want to help you."

"Help me do what?"

"Feel safe."

I was silent. I was silent a lot during the sessions that followed; sometimes so silent, she handed me a pad and paper and urged me to write. "Can you draw a picture for me?" she would ask.

"Of what?"

"Of somebody who makes you feel safe."

"What do you mean by 'safe?'"

"Like if someone was touching you in a way you didn't want them to, or hurting you, or scaring you or something, who would you turn to? Who would you tell?"

"Who told you about me?" I would ask at the end of every session.

"I can't say," Yolanda demurred. "Somebody who cares." I wondered which of the men I was seeing, slamming into, would be resourceful enough to look up the number of her hotline. I wasn't sure if I wanted to love this man or resent the hell out of him.

"I need to know," I insisted.

"It's confidential. Someone who thought you were at risk."

"At risk." I didn't know what that meant either. It sounded dire and drab, strangely impersonal.

Finally, when the obligatory number of sessions ended, Yolanda said, "Be careful." She shook my hand and offered her business card.

"Who told you about me?" Surely she could tell me now.

She looked pained. "The message landed in your box by accident. It was actually meant for someone else."

"You must be joking."

"Someone who has the same initials."

She was right: the original message was addressed simply to "J. T."

"Why didn't you say anything?" I demanded to know. We had been there under such resoundingly false pretenses.

"You seemed troubled. I thought you needed help."

But I was beyond help, tattooed more by my isolation than my own initials. I threw her card away even before I reached my car. I didn't request a referral, or drug therapy, or a support group, nor did I seek out the other "J. T.," who was also suffering. I was as oblivious to her struggle as I was hardened to my own pain.

23.

One day the phone in my office at the Taper rang.

"Jessie, it's me. I want to see you."

Joe. How did he find me now, so long after my escape?

I remembered meeting him at Rockefeller Center in midwinter, little girls clicking past in their holiday heels, families cuddling in the cold, too-big ornaments on a too-big tree. It was too late to care about him, to figure him out. I had to keep moving.

Don't look back.

You can never look back.

"You can only do one thing for me," I said after a moment. "Never, never call me again."

PART FOUR

THE CHOSEN
AND THE LOST

Man hands on misery to man,
It deepens like a coastal shelf.
                    —Philip Larkin

24.

I always thought I would marry a man with a beard, who was tall and smart and funny. Michael seemed to be all that. We were fixed up by a friend, who said Michael was a partner at one of the city's most liberal law firms. She also said he didn't have much hair. I didn't care about the hair, and I liked that he had worked for a public interest law group and on a gun control campaign.

But it took Michael a long time to call. And I was late to our first date, which he realized later should have indicated a pattern. (Luckily, he did not realize it then.)

More uncharacteristic was my silence at the table, but I was nervous—so nervous, I spent the entire meal drawing pictures on the tablecloth of everything he talked about: his house with sixty-three steps, his vintage car, the cat he hoped to have when he wasn't working nights and weekends and holidays. I invited him to my thirtieth birthday party later that week, but he said he was taking his young niece skiing. Knowing he'd been a philosophy major, I attempted some awful pun about "skiing and nothingness," a disaster, and not only because he hated Sartre.

Still, at the end of our first date, Michael asked me out again.

"I could be very interested in this man," I told my mother on the phone after that first dinner.

And I thought he could be interested in me.

When he leaned in to kiss me after our second date, in the underground parking lot below his office in Century City, I turned away, and he laughed, saying he didn't mean to be forward.

But the fact that I didn't want to kiss him on that second date—or the third, or the fourth—should have signaled something about my readiness for intimacy.

Yet Michael seemed unfazed. It was awkward, but he had a high tolerance for awkwardness: when I cut him off mid-sentence, when I frowned at a joke.

He was wonderful. He even saved the tablecloth from that first date, on which I'd drawn pictures of his longed-for cat and vintage Corvette, and made it into a thirtieth birthday card, sending it to me with a bottle of champagne.

But I still didn't want to kiss him. I felt toxic, and I didn't want to hurt him, to ruin his remarkable buoyancy. He was the most optimistic smart person I'd ever met.

Michael always seemed in command, insisting on another table at a nice restaurant if we were seated too close to the kitchen. He assembled his own bouquets at Whole Foods, to the bemusement of the shop clerk, because he thought he could do it as well as any florist on Rodeo Drive. He decided to leave litigation for entertainment law, and he wore his celebrity clientele lightly: He didn't party with the actors he represented, or pamper them. He knew they were good people, and he spoke to their best selves, as he did to mine. "Don't wound anyone you can't kill," Michael would tell me. I was always judging other people, for fear of being judged. But Michael, to his great credit, wasn't judging *anyone*, let alone wounding them.

He felt as at home in the world as I was uneasy in my own skin.

The night he proposed, we were lying in bed, reading different sections of *The New York Times*, when he inquired, "If I were to ask you to marry me, would you say yes?" I was so nervous, I resorted to diagramming his proposal. Was he using the future pluperfect or the past subjunctive? *Was he asking me to marry him?* That moment has remained a source of contention to this day, as has our wedding cake. I didn't realize he hated cakes with fruit.

When we took our vows at a private ranch in Malibu, two horses cavorted in a field behind us. For years people would call us on our anniversary, remembering that image, in all its beauty and surprise. But the love between us wasn't volatile, barely controlled, like those horses, and that was good, I thought.

I would not be suffocated or effaced.

25.

On our honeymoon, we went to Anguilla, an eel-shaped island (hence its name), and then to Ireland. Anguilla was luxurious and intimidating: all that intimacy, as potentially suffocating as the billowing curtains that cocooned the bed.

There was a wonderful little restaurant called Hibernia, run by an Irish cook and his charming wife. It was strange to have two bona fide Irish people to talk to on this little Caribbean island, about all that lay ahead of us in the coming weeks, when we headed to Ireland. Shelagh and Donal suggested we drive to Connemara, the rocky western coast, where the stone walls are built with holes in them, to let the wind race through. I loved the idea of something so solid, so ancient, that acknowledged in its very structure the need for release.

"You must go visit my friend in Dublin," Shelagh urged me. "She runs a sweet little shop off Francis Street. Sells wonderful lingerie, lacy stuff, the real Irish lace." Her voice had the warmth and darkness of a genuine lager. What was an Irish couple doing on a little island off the coast of Puerto Rico, a sliver of coral and limestone with a single traffic light?

"Maybe they're smugglers," Michael mused, as we readied

for bed in our little villa. The place was spackled with geckos, and we could hear them racing each other up and down the walls throughout the night. In the morning, a pot of strong, dark coffee appeared outside our door, along with freshly baked croissants nestled in a native basket. It was all impossibly romantic, and a little overwhelming, too. We lay in bed, talking about the charming Irish couple. What could they be smuggling? Drugs? Lobsters? Lingerie?

Two nights later, when we went back for dinner, Shelagh told me, "You'll love my friend in Dublin. She's darling. And the clothes are gorgeous. Little cammies—what do you Americans call them? Camisoles?"

The Irish could say anything and make it sound desirable— "tarantula," "chlamydia"—but the word "camisole" was particularly mellifluous.

"I'm not a lingerie girl," I wanted to say. But why wasn't I? I didn't want to do anything—*wear* anything—that might seem provocative. If Michael loved me, really loved me, he wouldn't *want* me too much. The only sex I knew was galvanizing, terrifying. I hoped he would not ask for that.

I *chose* him because he wouldn't ask for that. Because we weren't drawn to each other that way. Yet we cuddled in bed, making each other laugh, speculating about our Irish friends. What were they doing in Anguilla? Were they in some kind of trouble? Was it the Troubles themselves?

Our next stop was Ireland, where neither of us had ever been. We had the typical difficulty driving on the "wrong" side of the road. The task was made more challenging by my insistence on stopping every time we saw an animal wander into traffic. By the end of the day, I was shepherding whole flocks of sheep across the sinuous lanes.

The next day, we drove up to a lovely Georgian house, and

I knocked on the door. "Are we too late for tea?" I inquired as politely as I could. "I've already had my tea," said the elderly woman who answered the door, looking at me quizzically. It turns out the actual tea shop was located in the next town.

But the most misguided moment took place in our hotel in County Cork when, in the midst of a terrible fight, I removed my wedding ring and threw it across the room. The next day, we glowered at each other over the much-vaunted Irish breakfast, complete with sheep brain sausage and a tomato from the Pleistocene age. Each table was reserved for a visiting couple, their name on a card tucked into a little vase of sweet peas. Ours said "Gender 2." "Gender" was a misspelling of "Gendler," Michael's last name. But in a way, that little sign encapsulated our problems. Not that we were two different genders. We were too *different*, in every possible way.

In Oxford, I took Michael to the Wyckham tea shop, where Liam had lifted me, our reflection caught in the storefront's watery glass. Michael was so tall, and the tea shop so tiny, that he kept knocking over the decorative cups and saucers, while I kept retrieving them. I had loved Oxford, and I couldn't wait to share the medieval city with him. But both of us seemed out of place: He, so absurdly tall; and me, seemingly daffy. He was Gulliver. I was Lucille Ball.

Over cucumber sandwiches, I told him about the day I met the Queen, at the end of my time at Oxford, when the Rhodes Trust held a party to celebrate its first 80 years. She was resplendent —"gorgeous," Shelagh would say—in a blinding yellow suit and gloves and hat. She looked like a giant tennis ball. "You mustn't look at her unless she looks at you first," we were instructed. "You mustn't extend your hand. If she speaks to you, you may respond, but only then." The young Rhodes women were encouraged to wear gloves. We talked at length about whether we should curtsey—we were, after all, dissidents, colonists. Was the bended knee a gesture of obeisance or respect? And what would we talk about if she spoke to us?

"Begin by calling her 'Your Majesty,'" the Rhodes secretary said. "In any follow-up, you must refer to her as 'Ma'am.'" I couldn't imagine speaking to her at all, let alone engaging in a conversation that involved a follow-up. What would I ask her? "Why, Your Majesty, are you always clutching a purse?" I later learned the Queen only carries money on Sundays, so she can place a bill in the church collection box, which is very generous of her, very down to earth. Although apparently she has a footman who irons the bill beforehand, folding it so her picture faces upward. (Her picture is on all the money, after all.)

I did not talk to the Queen about her purse, or to Shelagh about the Troubles. I did not talk to Michael about all that was troubling me. There was so much we shared: sympathy and recognition and a love of chocolate and Cézanne's apples. Wasn't that enough for me? For him?

Nor, in the end, did I seek out the little lingerie shop in Dublin. I didn't want to provoke something confounding, intemperate. If he loved me, really loved me, he would let me keep my clothes on.

I would try to keep my wedding ring on as well.

I would try, every day—even all these years later—to find another reason for choosing Michael and the life we'd made. Yet twenty years on, it still surprises me to read "Malibu" on my marriage license and "Los Angeles" on the birth certificates of our two girls. It's as if I fell asleep next to a pool and awakened, disoriented, after decades of slumber, letting the sun and the stillness suction away my youth. I wanted to reinvent myself, and for that, Los Angeles was legendarily hospitable. Everything here was up for grabs. Nothing seemed to last: Not hillsides. Not production deals. Not marriages.

But mine had. Nearly twenty years. Yet there was always a tension, something trembling just below the surface, distancing me from the material world of happiness, of home. Prompting me to do stupid things, dangerous things, that could put my entire world at risk.

Like saying "yes" when Anthony invited me to lunch.

26.

⤲

Anthony was a beguiling mix of outlaw and aesthete. He had been my first boyfriend at Yale. He drank French-pressed coffee and knew who Derrida was, or at least he said he did, and that impressed me, as did the fact that he had ridden from San Francisco to New Haven on a motorcycle while the rest of us tumbled from our mothers' station wagons, armed with the requisite down comforter and matching sheets. Anthony and I dated awkwardly but passionately as freshmen, then parted company. We did not stay in touch.

But, sixteen years later, when he saw me walking on Montana Avenue, cradling baby Isabel, he grabbed my arm and invited me to lunch.

The following week, we sat across from each other at the 17th Street Café and reminisced about our courtship, and when the bill arrived, he said his truck had broken down and asked if I could give him a lift. Outside his apartment, he leaned in.

"Can I kiss you?"

I wanted to say, *Are you kidding? I'm lactating!*

But I just said "no."

But we started to spend time together and I was drawn in,

again, by his sophistication. He spoke French and wrote poems on his laptop, including a poem for me. He read it to me as we lay too close to each other on the sand at Zuma Beach.

"Can I kiss you?"

"No," I said. Kissing for me had always been a big deal.

But soon I was curled up next to Anthony in his battered truck, kissing him, moving against him, or lying on the floor of his apartment as he read to me from *The Hitchhiker's Guide to the Galaxy*.

I kissed him and it seemed like it might go farther; *I* might go farther.

"Don't cross the line," a friend warned. "You can never come back."

Finally, reluctantly, I told Anthony, "We've got to stop seeing each other. It's too confusing."

"But I want you." That's all he said. What did *I* want? Something propulsive and dangerous and disruptive, like the "seismic event" that was forever imminent in Southern California, requiring everyone to keep an earthquake supply kit in her trunk. But the frisson I got—when Anthony touched me, kissed me—was no tectonic shift. It was hardly a tremor. It was confirmation of how stuck we were. In his case, *literally* stuck, since he had nothing to move him: no job or spouse or kids. Even his truck had been repossessed.

I stopped seeing Anthony, and I vowed never to speak of him to Michael. But I thought about him all the time. He had said, unabashedly, *I want you*. What *did* I want?

To be close to Michael, like the couple in the Wallace Stevens poem we loved:

She wanted nothing . . .
. . . His arms would be her necklace.

Instead I was longing for Anthony, even as I knew I was blackening the foundations of the only home where I ever felt safe.

* * *

Months later, Michael suggested we take a family trip to Hawaii. We ate macadamia nut pancakes and watched a tiny scorpion scuttle across the floor. One day he invited me to go on a hike and took me to a spot that looked lush and foreboding.

I was a little nervous, and the passel of signs warning us to KEEP OUT didn't help.

But I followed him into the undergrowth, our breathing growing more labored as we climbed, past signs that blared OFF LIMITS, past an elfin man on a rock who wagged his finger at us. Higher and higher, past jacaranda and frangipani, the fragrance almost overpowering, or maybe it was the heat, or the proximity to Michael, after so many months of feeling disengaged.

At the top of the mountain, we stumbled upon an ancient site, home to a hula school, back when hula was a sacred practice, the province of men. All that remained was a semicircle of shrines, hulking and decrepit, laden with offerings: bougainvillea branches and orange peels and stones.

Michael and I separated in silence. After a moment, we each placed an offering on a shrine.

What was he wishing for? I wondered. He didn't often do things like this.

I was wishing I had never met Anthony.

I said a prayer at the top of the mountain, not for myself or for Michael, but for Isabel, asleep at the hotel with a babysitter nearby. *Let her be freer than I am, let her feel safe, let her know love without torment.*

Let her know who she is. Let her know what she wants.

Michael walked toward me, and we met in the center of the circle, the shrines guarding us like elders. As he drew me close, I could smell the scent of the ocean on his neck, mingled with the fragrance of the oranges and the incense. It was the first time we had touched in a very long time.

"Please forgive me," I whispered, not even knowing I was going to say it.

He smiled and drew me in closer and said, "Of course."

But I found it very hard to forgive myself for what happened, or *almost* happened. Had I betrayed him? What if I strayed again? I worried about it every time I looked at the scar on my foot, where I'd cut myself on a jagged cowrie shell; a scar shaped like a lightning bolt. Like the jolt I had given my marriage, hoping to destroy it. As if the only sensation I could tolerate was the feeling of being ensnared. Off-center, out of kilter, unbalanced, prey to exposure, about to be buffeted, battered. Those feelings were home. What Michael offered was something I had never felt: the warmth of real recognition. Nothing could be more unfamiliar, unforeseen. "Your family's crest," he once said, "could have had a very simple motto: You are totally on your own."

But he wanted me, and he wouldn't let me go.

27.

Lacey's fidelity to her fears, her demons, had brought her brother tremendous heartbreak. Why wouldn't she let him in? Had she been afraid to reveal any crack in her alabaster perfection? So much so that she would rather die? It was a sobering thought.

"I've lost people in a lot of ways, but suicide is so painful," Kyle told me. "The idea that they chose not to go to you. This was a choice, not to trust you or love you enough to let you help them." His anguish at not being able to reach her had a residual urgency. I could feel him missing her still.

Yet I understood how hard it was to let people in, even Michael. Growing up, I'd never had a sense that anyone was poised to help me. Who would that have been? A teacher? A dancer in the company? I wanted someone to *sense* that I was in trouble, from the bruises and crying bouts, the tortured poems strewn around my room. But I never said anything. This longing to be saved was perhaps my truest link to Lacey. Yet her silence confounded me; her unwillingness to be touched. This was the mystery that most needed solving: why she never asked for help, and neither did I.

A few weeks later, Kyle sent me an email:

As for Corinne and Simon, I have contacted them both and they are receptive to speaking with you. In fact, my sister was very anxious to speak with you. She was upset that I didn't give her your phone number. So, if you want to call her instead of emailing, her number is . . . I hope she doesn't get too worked up.

"Too worked up." What did he mean? Because Corinne thought Lacey had been murdered? Would I be able to talk to her about that? But before I could approach her, Corinne pre-empted me by calling Anson Bishop, Lacey's colleague at Chatsworth, to question him about me. Anson then called me out of the blue.

"Get back to me, sooner rather than later," his message urged. When I finally reached him, he changed course entirely, saying it was "nothing," he didn't have time to talk, he was getting on a plane, he would "get in trouble" if he scheduled any conversations on his own. He told me I would need to arrange something with his secretary, then mumbled an email address for her that proved impossible to compute.

According to Kyle, it was Anson who brought Lacey to Chatsworth; both had done their DPhils at Oxford, completing their degrees with distinction. "The only conversations I've had with him were clinical," Kyle told me. "I think Chatsworth was afraid they'd be implicated. We live in a very litigious society. There were others who might have jumped."

Other people who suffered as Lacey had. Did she try to counsel them, comfort them? Why, despite the beautifully cadenced obituary in the *Oxonian,* were there so few people to talk to about her?

Anson had nothing to offer, not even viable contact information. On to Corinne.

28.

But first, I asked Michael about Anson.

"What good is contact information if you can't use it to contact someone?" he wondered, with characteristic clarity.

"Should I keep trying to get in touch with him?"

"I wouldn't. But then, I wouldn't be doing any of this."

"This," to Michael, was an indulgence, a diversion, taking me ever further from him, our daughters, and the dog.

"You seem less happy than before. More preoccupied."

"But the research is interesting. Did you know many coroners won't buy a two-storey house? They know how hard it is to lug a body down a flight of stairs . . . "

"Why would I need to know that?" he asked, more weary than impatient. "How is it helping you?"

"It's helping, but I don't know how."

We were walking along Wilshire Boulevard, wanting to hold hands but failing, never quite having found the right position for hand-holding, even though we had been together more than twenty years. We noticed a surprising number of shops had been shuttered: the print shop, the florist, the vintage clothing store. Even the little café on the corner was gone.

"These days you can buy pretty much anything online," Michael said. "That's easier. And people want what's easy, don't they?"

"Is there anything that's not better being virtual?" I wondered.

He looked at me intently and said, "You."

I *wanted* to be real, to make something happen between us, surprising and powerful and tender, not tentative. Not in the dark, but in the half-light, the violet hour, where past and present converge, his breath mingling with mine.

Yet there I was, lying in bed at night, hoping he wouldn't touch me. Breathing a sigh of relief when snoring signaled he had yielded to sleep. Frozen, unable to move, waiting as he wanted to enter me. Tears streaming down my face, but silently, so he wouldn't suspect.

I think certain people are most themselves when they are having sex. I was one of those people, or could have been. To have that smashed, hijacked by someone else's brutality, is a kind of death.

"Oh, sweetheart," Michael would murmur into my neck.

But I was still in bed with Joe.

He was on top of me, in a bed besieged, dirty clothing everywhere, cigarette butts making a mosaic of the floor. Jenny the dog would whine, but I tried not to cry out as Joe labored, trying to get me to feel pleasure, to pleasure him.

"You fucking cunt," he would say, feeling me retreat.

"Joe, please stop it. Please."

"I could kill you, you fucking cunt. I could kill you."

I was sure he would.

Joe had offered me an escape, and I had taken it, only to find myself trapped in a different dungeon: nails ripping through his attic roof, his hand plunging inside me, his teeth on my nipple, on my neck.

It was like being in a coffin, except a coffin would have been safer. In a coffin, I would have been alone. Here, there was Joe, lusting, pumping, groaning, rutting like a malevolent machine.

"I could kill you, you fucking cunt."

But I was already dead. Or worse: I had been buried alive.

While Michael slept, I would have to awaken the part of me that went dead back then, the part that feared to show itself, to make itself known. I hadn't died; I had survived, and created this life with Michael. If only I could make his arms my necklace; his embrace, my shield.

29.

What thrust me into Joe's arms when I was much younger was a feeling that I was not truly female. He saw me as a woman—as I had never been seen. But before long, my body felt like a crime scene, only there was no yellow police tape around it. There was no excavation, no release. There was no way to go from what happened with Joe into something loving and nurturing with another man. I wanted the screaming, the brokenness, and then I wanted out.

I often felt I tempted men to mishandle me because I didn't really want contact. I didn't want to be known. I didn't want to learn about myself, about someone else, in those sweaty, secret moments. I wanted someone to obliterate me.

Then Isabel came into my life, and the baby redeemed the beating. For the first time, I felt whole. When I nursed her, the milk rushed through me like a filament, drawing us closer. It was the first bond that felt like it might strengthen, not strangle, me.

But for a long time, I was reluctant to have another child.

"Two kids feels like a family," Michael kept saying.

"Let's wait until they finish painting the kitchen," was all I could say.

I couldn't tell Michael the truth: I was afraid to lose myself completely in a process that was so consuming, to make someone less compelling than Isabel.

When she was three, Isabel looked up at the sky—the moon was very close—and asked, "What happens if there's no gravity?" I think she wanted to know, "How are we all connected? Can we float away?" She loved bats and was aggrieved that they were often menaced and misunderstood. Sometimes she would tell dinner guests that if a bat were starving, another bat would regurgitate food into its mouth (which always put a bit of a damper on our meal). And once, when a dead mouse landed in our front garden, she bent down very close to it and sniffed it. She was very brave, very different from me.

Then, of course, when I was finally ready to conceive, I could not get pregnant. Every month when my period came, I wept. I felt again what I had felt as an adolescent, when I attracted interest from a man I didn't want: My body was betraying me. It didn't want me to do this, and yet all around me were women, glorious, round, radiant, cooing to their babies or passing them off to nannies in the park. I was forty, then forty-one. We made the rounds to fertility doctors, trying a variety of expensive and humiliating strategies, including timed intercourse and artificial insemination.

One doctor handed me a drawing of the female reproductive system, on which he scrawled a grim prediction: 3 percent chance of having a live birth.

The fact that infertile women have the same rates of depression as women dying of cancer did not surprise me at all.

I booked weekly visits to the Jewish acupuncturist with the dangly earrings, who kept telling me, "There's a baby hovering over you." This would have been annoying if it hadn't been so intriguing. What was the hovering baby *doing* up there? It seemed unsafe to use needles when the hovering baby was circling. I didn't want to puncture her.

I even consulted a palm reader, who said there was another baby waiting for me, then asked if my husband knew Barbra Streisand and could score tickets for her farewell tour. I went to see a psychic who asked me, before our session started, if I needed to use the bathroom. If he were truly psychic, my husband later reasoned, wouldn't he have *known?*

I'd begun to see a counselor who specialized in matching infertile couples with egg donors. My husband was happy to use someone else's egg. "One less person related to your family," he would say, only half-joking.

One day, as I was leaving her office, I noticed women entering the celebrated clinic across the hall. I had been a patient there once, so I stopped in. Nothing about the place had changed, except that on the front counter, next to the sign-in sheet and the hand sanitizer, was an article about a procedure called GIFT. It turned out that GIFT had been replaced by in vitro fertilization, which was less invasive and didn't require a general anesthetic. But it had advantages over in vitro: the egg and sperm were mixed together in the operating room and re-implanted, returning immediately to a natural environment. It seemed like a subtle difference, but it might be critical: the embryo could float down on its own, and attach to the wall of the womb.

The next day I made my way downtown to the clinic where I actually *was* a patient. A young doctor was scarfing down a piece of cold pizza in the tiny kitchenette.

"Can I talk to you for a moment?"

"Sure," he muttered between bites.

"Would this work?" I asked, holding up the article on GIFT. "I only have one more chance."

"Maybe," he said, chewing his pizza thoughtfully. "It may be that the fertilized egg looks good when we put it back in. On the screen it looks like it's being deposited perfectly. But microscopically the body is rejecting it. GIFT would avoid that."

"Can we try it?"

"No one does it anymore. It's not safe. It involves a general and a surgical incision and all."

"I'd be willing to try it," I said, not having consulted my husband, nor even the palm reader, never having scored those Streisand tickets for her.

Days later, after the procedure, the embryologist told me she had placed seven eggs into one fallopian tube and the eighth into the other.

"Why only one in the other tube?" I asked, groggy and unsure of my math.

She smiled. "One of the eggs escaped. It didn't want to go up the tube with the others. It went up the other tube instead."

I tried to imagine the egg, intrepid, venturing up the other passage, when one of the nurses handed me a saltine. I ate it without even bothering to wash my hands, despite all my phobias, and I had just used the bathroom, a *hospital* bathroom, without a protective covering on the seat. For me, it was a moment as seismic as the conversion of Paul, only it involved sedation and a stale saltine.

Charlotte, ever the adventurer, was born nine months later. (She had a great sense of direction, and still does.) The saltine was my manna, and Charlotte, my one good egg, venturing into the other tube, alone but undeterred. The Buddhists believe our children choose us, to teach us, to free us. Maybe Charlotte had been waiting for me to let go. "What if there's no gravity?" Isabel had asked, but Charlotte let gravity pull her in, floating beauty. Charlotte knew how to connect.

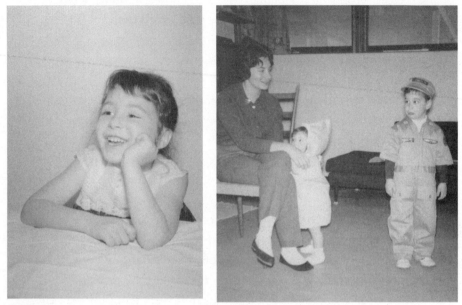

Age five

With my mother and older brother, Douglas

With my father and younger brother, Roger, in front of the house my mother designed

Dancing in high school, 1977

At Yale, 1981

With my brothers Roger (left) and Douglas (right), 1964

With my brothers, 1990

Yale graduation, with my father, mother and maternal grandfather, 1981

With my mother at Oxford, 1983

On the set of Directing Workshop for Women film, 1990

At the Mark Taper Forum, 1988

Our wedding in Malibu, 1991

With Isabel in the Berkshires, 1997

With Michael and Isabel in Hawaii, 1996

Charlotte and Isabel, 2001

Isabel, Michael and Charlotte, Santa Barbara, 2005

Isabel and Charlotte, Napa, 2007

Isabel and one of many caution signs

Isabel, Michael, and the feral pig warning

My mother, with dog and book

Emma

With Charlotte after the Rhodes celebration, 2008

Isabel and Charlotte, dancing in a field near Oxford

30.

The doctor who delivered Charlotte had a kind of gnomic stability, even charm. He would say things like "Unluckiest is he without a psychic wound," a peculiar Zen koan to launch when your patient's feet are in stirrups, legs spread. But he was right: the wound is the way in, and we are wired for connection. It is density, intimacy, that keeps us safe. As Jennifer Senior has observed, evolutionary scientists believe loneliness—like hunger—sets off an internal alarm, reminding us to move closer. Otherwise, we would not survive.

Maybe that's why Lacey killed herself, because she didn't feel part of something bigger, an equation less bounded than even her brain could grasp. Or maybe Lacey killed herself because life is messy, gelatinous. She liked to control things. Life cannot be controlled. The things we crave—acceptance or forgiveness—are as little understood as rules to the game of cricket, or why the Queen always carries a purse. There is no reckoning, I know that now. There is no way to add it all up. There is only relief that we have come through, like the moments after a birth, when the world seems transparent, marvelous; when there is only blood and clarity and exhaustion and gratitude.

I wanted to let go, to move closer, or at least, I *thought* I did. But I still shivered when someone asked me to taste her entrée or sample his wine. If my seatmate sneezed, even a short plane trip could seem more grueling than the Iditarod. I wanted to be closer—in the abstract.

Frequently, stress would trigger my fears, and a conversation would quickly degenerate. No matter the provocation, the anger was always the same.

"You let her do it?"

"What?" Michael was sweaty and stunned, just off the tennis court.

"Eat the banana. The one in your tennis bag."

"Bananas are good for her. Charlotte's six. She's supposed to be eating more fruit."

"That banana was in the house when they fumigated."

"They fumigated the house *next door*. We're not living there."

"But all the studies show that fumes from those pesticides don't necessarily . . . " I couldn't think of the word, I was getting so upset. "Dissipate! They don't necessarily dissipate!"

"Of course they do."

"They have evidence. They've found evidence of those pesticides on rugs and carpets and bedspreads years later."

"I don't believe it."

"Why would I lie about it?"

"I don't think you're lying." He paused for a moment. "I think you're *nuts*."

"Because I'm trying to protect her?"

"Because it doesn't matter. All these things you worry about. Whatever it is that makes the ingredients in the ice cream stick together. Whether the bath toys are leaching plastic. It doesn't matter. There'd be no one left on the planet if it did."

"You'll see. It's like smoking. Or cell phones."

"I don't think she's smoking."

"Everybody thought *they* were safe. Then studies came out, suppressed by the powerful lobbies, that linked them to cancer."

"No banana has ever been linked to cancer. I can promise you that."

"Michael!"

"As Freud would say, sometimes a banana is just a banana."

"And sometimes you can be careless. And mean."

"Why? Because I don't want to raise a child in your world?"

"Because you didn't give me a chance to protect her."

"I don't want her to think that everything is terrifying." Anger was rising in him like rainwater. "Everything isn't toxic."

"But some things *are.*"

"But they're never the things you worry about."

He swung his tennis bag over his shoulder, with a vehemence I had rarely seen in him.

"Besides, nothing is more toxic than this fear."

He was right, but I couldn't admit it—to him or to myself. Almost thirty years after Joe, suspicion still bristled beneath every utterance. Paranoia crouched behind the sofa, waiting to pounce. I knew I was safe, I was loved, I had survived Joe. I was a "survivor." I had gotten myself away from him. And from my parents, and their house near the harbor, but I continued to dwell there. Maybe that's where the expression "don't dwell on it" came from. I didn't want to live there anymore. I wanted to live *here,* the afternoon light filtering through the canyons. That's what drew me to L.A., out of the shadows. All that light. But fear had planted itself in the loam of my life, in the very soil, braided itself around my happiness, like a strong weed strangling a tree. Michael was right. The fear was toxic. And fear was the very core of who I was.

That's what drew me to Lacey, wasn't it? That was the source of our kinship. That fear. We'd made our way across borders, across boundaries, but the fear had slipped into our baggage. It *was* our baggage. We had nothing to declare, except the fear. We were junkies, hooked on the perpetual high of panic. Anxiety was our hallucinogen. But when I spoke to Corinne, I wanted to seem calm, controlled, respectful. Given what Kyle had said, the conversation might be trip-wired. I had to watch my step.

Corinne was expecting my call, and her voice was flinty, hard at the edges, as if she had lived an eternity.

"We grew up in a very, very difficult childhood. Did Kyle tell you about that?"

"He told me about your stepfather, Robert. He said he was a prick."

"You mean my husband, Robert?"

"No, your stepfather. Wasn't his name Robert?"

"Oh, you mean Bob. I thought you meant he said my husband was a prick."

And so it began. From the first, I felt on the wrong foot, trying to win her trust by showing I knew something about her past, but mixing up Robert and Bob. Going forward, I would be careful not to seem too familiar. I just needed to let her talk.

"My father was an alcoholic. He physically abused my mother. Never touched his children. I was the oldest, four years older than Lacey. I tried to protect them by putting them in their rooms.

"My mom was emotionally, sexually abused as a child. Then she had twenty years with my father, he abused her, broke her arms, everything. My mom had a history of depression.

"My father finally left in '82, when I went to UCSD." Corinne was always offering me dates, as if to verify events for which her word was sufficient. Or perhaps the dates helped her to root herself.

"So I didn't really have a stepfather. I was already gone. I was always in trouble, grounded. Lacey escaped through books. She would check out five books from the library and read them all. She became an overachiever. I didn't study. I got As and Bs and that was fine.

"My father was my best friend." She laughed a flat, coarse laugh, without energy. "He was taken from me, too. You know, there's no such thing as closure. Your life just becomes manageable. My dad. He stopped taking his heart medication. He had a heart attack a year and a half later. He just gave up."

Her torrent of words slowed, and I found myself asking, incredulously: "Your dad was your best friend, even though you saw him break your mother's arms?"

"I had made my peace with my father years before."

Conversation with Corinne was a roller coaster of bluster, suspicion, introspection, recrimination, and regret. "I've been sober since November 15, 1993. I was in AA," she told me. "I had serenity and all that stuff. Lacey was one of the first people Chatsworth hired who didn't have an MBA. She was really stressed out. She said, 'I can't wait to come back to California. You and I can have a close relationship again. You can help me get more calm and more serene.'"

Then Corinne veered away from the reflective to something concrete and differently revealing: "After her death, Chatsworth ended that program. They were having them do a mini-MBA in a month. It was incredibly stressful. Especially for someone who wasn't a mathematician."

Lacey couldn't measure up. That was a constant refrain. She couldn't do the math. Maybe she realized that charm wasn't going to help with the late nights and harsh critiques, the brutal pace and unrelenting pressure. No algorithm could make those elements cohere.

What made her take a job at Chatsworth rather than a post in academia? She was married to a scholar; she didn't seem interested in money. Was it just another challenge to master, another pinnacle?

Before I could ask, Corinne was on to another subject. "England was dark, dank, dreary. Lacey was always stressed. She never felt she was good enough. I don't know, maybe you know, how many women, or men even, are Rhodes, Truman, and Fulbright scholars."

I remarked on how extraordinary those accomplishments were, and Corinne agreed. "It's amazing what she could have become, what she *had* become, at such an early age. She was wanting to get on a calm path. I was going to help."

Here was the real poignancy: Corinne had something to offer her accomplished little sister, and she never got the chance. Or was Lacey being generous to her? Did she really think Corinne could help her find her way?

"Then, suddenly, I didn't have a sister. Do you have a sister?"

"No."

"You don't have anyone to share things with: the first baby, the first job promotion."

Corinne was quiet for a moment. "Brothers are not the same."

Her words made me think of my daughters, each, happily, with a sister. But what did sisterhood really mean? It seemed to involve a bond more complex and inviolate than the swapping of hair products or nail art. Maybe, in its best moments, a sense of otherness melted away. I never had any close female friends in high school, or even at Yale. I didn't know what women talked about. They seemed mysterious, alluring, the possessors of secrets as filmy as nylons. I had grown up in the brawling, careless world of boys.

My first real experience of sisterhood was in Lamaze class, when I was pregnant with Isabel. I met a woman who seemed like a character out of a Beverly Cleary novel, with her strong Midwestern features and sturdiness. We became friends, and slowly we collected other new mothers, all with infant daughters the same age as ours. Over the years we evolved into a book group, even when we gave up reading books. We saw each other through many crises: a divorce, a bout with cancer, a child's mysterious illness. We talked about everything from presidential politics (based on our non-reading of *John Adams*) to whether Uma Thurman's breasts were real (ditto: *The Golden Bowl*).

I knew that both my daughters had friends to whom they felt as close as sisters. I hoped they would share the bond Corinne was gesturing at.

Then again, sisterhood didn't save Lacey. She wouldn't let anyone in to ease her pain.

Maybe if I'd had a sister, I might not have been so vulnerable to Joe. I could have confided in her when he pummeled me. I hoped one day my daughters would trust each other more, tell each other everything. Help each other, as Lacey's siblings did not.

31.

Several weeks later, we went to the beach to celebrate *Tashlich*, the ceremony just after the Jewish New Year, when people throw pieces of bread into the water to cast away their sins. Isabel was wearing her new bright blue bikini. I, as ever, was dressed in black, like a character out of Chekhov or Charles Addams. Everyone else seemed to be wearing white, a tribute to the newness of the year. An Ethiopian drummer pounded out a beat, as beachgoers banged on their Tupperware.

"Here," I told Isabel. "Take this piece of bread."

"I'm a Buddhist," she said with her best tween insolence. "I might even be Bahá'í."

Her friend Julia, all sandy beauty and insouciance, looked at her quizzically. Charlotte crept toward the water, daring the waves to catch the hem of her pants.

"Don't go too far," I shouted to Isabel, as she and Julia ventured into the waves. Victoria, Julia's mother, and I took turns watching them. She talked about a mutual friend whose husband cheated on her but lied, saying he was on a film set in South Korea. (He was actually in bed with a woman in Koreatown.)

"That's the kind of thing we're not supposed to be talking about today," I said. "Or ever."

"Adultery?" Victoria smiled. "It's as old as the ceremony of *Tashlich*."

"But it's always the men you don't think will stray, who seem stable or schlumpy. He was so schlumpy."

"And he hated animals. She was always having to take the guinea pigs out of the house. He hated the noise."

"Whose guinea pigs?" Charlotte asked. She wanted a mother who'd let her have a rodent, a mother who wasn't me.

When I expressed my sense of inadequacy, Victoria chided me. "*That's* the kind of thing you're not supposed to say. Not ever. It frightens the kids."

"She knows I'm kidding," I countered. "At least, I hope she does." *More bread, please*—I had committed yet another misstep—and a handsome stranger handed over a roll.

I began to shred it. I did regret saying those things, even thinking them. I wished I could be more resilient, more secure. "Just keep moving," someone counseled me once, but I had been in limbo for such a long time. Not peaceful, not hopeful, not *here*.

Again, I thought of Lacey, and I realized: It was more than a sense of inadequacy that linked us. It was a feeling of loss bordering on despair. Maybe that feeling pre-dated Joe, even primed me for him. No matter: I thought I hid it well. Other people thought I was happy—or at least, contented. Or at least, I *thought* they did. But my children needed me to be so much more. They needed me to let go of the past, a past that purled around them like seawater. My children needed me to be brave. Maybe it was true, as I once read, that some part of our children stays in our bodies long after we give birth to them. Then part of our story must be part of their story, too. I had wished it away, buried it beneath fights with friends and the drama of deadlines. But the knot grew ever tighter. They could not breathe.

* * *

Charlotte splashed in the water, the bits of bread bobbing around her, a tiny flotilla of misbegotten wishes and regrets. She was too young to understand the ritual, but Isabel was not, and I wished she would embrace it.

"Where is Isabel?" I asked.

"She's down there with Julia," Victoria gestured.

"But where?"

"I don't know. I see Julia's head. I can always tell . . . "

"But where's Isabel?"

I grabbed Charlotte's hand and ran toward Julia. "Where's Isabel?"

"I don't know."

"Wasn't she with you?"

"Yeah. But she said she wanted to go and find her towel."

"Her towel's right here," I said.

"I'll keep Charlotte and you go look," Victoria offered.

"No. I don't . . . I can't. Charlotte, come with me. Come on, let's run."

We ran along the sand, growing more frantic. I spotted a lifeguard station with a young lifeguard, tanned and blond and slightly empty-looking.

I raced up the ramp, barefoot, tugging Charlotte behind me.

"My daughter's lost," I sobbed. "I can't find her."

"What was she wearing?"

"A bathing suit!"

"What color?"

"I don't know! I don't know!"

I couldn't believe I couldn't remember the color. Luckily, Charlotte piped up: "It was blue!"

"What does she look like?" the lifeguard asked.

"She's tall with dark hair and blue eyes. She has pale skin."

He lifted his binoculars and scanned the horizon. "I don't see her."

Charlotte began to cry.

"Please!" I shouted. "You've got to help me! She's a strong swimmer. I know she wouldn't have drowned."

"You don't have to worry about drowning," the lifeguard reassured us. "What you have to worry about is all the perverts on the beach."

"What's a pervert?" Charlotte asked through tears.

I didn't answer. I was too afraid. I would have thrown bread into the water forever to atone for this moment of negligence, of nonchalance. Joking with Victoria, thinking our daughters were splashing nearby, a process of approximation; thinking I saw her still. Would I ever see her again?

"Here are your shoes," Victoria said, reaching me, breathing heavily. Julia took Charlotte's hand, then dropped it, uncertain what to do. By now the ceremony had ended and the others had moved off, though some children lagged behind, eating bits of bread.

"Put them on," Victoria said. "Your feet are starting to bleed."

Charlotte began jumping up and down. "I see her! Isabel! Isabel!"

Isabel staggered toward us, exhausted.

"Oh my God, Isabel!" I could barely speak.

"Isabel, I love you!" Charlotte screamed, throwing her arms around Isabel's waist.

"I love you, too," Isabel said, quietly so her friend wouldn't hear.

"Where were you?!" I was too relieved to be furious.

"I thought I put my towel down in front of lifeguard station 41," she said, panting. "But there *is* no 41."

Charlotte was still hugging her. "You're a miracle!"

"And you're a nice person, Charlotte. If occasionally . . . *sticky*. That's onomatopoetic, isn't it?" Isabel looked at me and grinned.

I kissed her on the top of the head, her hair tangled like seaweed, the smell of the ocean on her, like strangeness, like otherness. She was so tall, her hair so wild, it obscured my view of the horizon. She was almost as tall as I was. I hadn't noticed that until now.

* * *

In the weeks that followed, I often thought back to that day at the beach. We had come so close to something unspeakable. "Minutes and inches," a friend once told me. "That's all life is." But there are other gaps between what we say and what we mean, between who we think we are and how we behave; forbidding gulfs where children—and trust and partnerships—can be lost.

"Life is a veil," a rabbi insisted at the funeral of a friend's toddler, who drowned in a hot tub, his tiny sneakers rigid in the cold night air. We sat *shiva* in the backyard, men in their long black coats, women keening, as other people's children idled, uncertain, near the swings. Michael and I didn't have kids yet, but our friends who did all seemed to have the same thought: It could have happened to them. We *all* have moments when we look away. "Life is a veil, and sometimes it tears and someone slips through," the rabbi said.

That someone might have been Isabel. But here she was, restored to me, sunburned but triumphant. She had weathered something fearsome, and survived.

Perhaps I needed to trust the world more, to see it as munificent—or at least, not menacing. "I must learn to be content," Jane Austen said, "with being happier than I deserve." But I would never forget the feeling that I had nearly lost her, through my own carelessness or the conspiracy of forces I had not dared imagine. There was no conspiracy. I was happier, *luckier,* than I deserved.

32.

Most of the time, the unpredictability of life made Michael *more* cheerful. He didn't think the world was menacing. "Other people always know more about us than we think they do," he would say, as if to reassure me. But I wondered: *Was that intimacy a comfort or a threat?*

I sensed that Corinne and I had this in common: a desire to be seen understood believed respected relied upon. And a suspicion that no one would ever see us. No one would ever understand. Years later, when I read about other survivors of sexual abuse, I was astonished to hear them say: "I didn't tell anyone because I didn't think anyone could help." They hid the screaming matches from neighbors; the bruises, from ER nurses. They sent the police away without filing a report. They wanted someone to help, but didn't trust anyone to understand the complexity of the situation; to see the connections, the lies and collusions and traps. They thought only they understood, and it was up to *them* to protect others—to protect *everyone*—even as they could not protect themselves.

So when Kyle told me about Corinne's suspicions, I understood them almost viscerally. Of course, the world was rigged. Still, I waited for her to broach the subject of conspiracy that seemed to roil beneath the surface. Finally, it erupted with a great force.

"I'm very different from my brother," she declared. "I'm not completely convinced my sister committed suicide."

"You're not?"

"Kyle thinks she was really depressed. But I saw her the day after her car accident. She wasn't depressed. I took her to Beverly Hills to see a dentist, to get her teeth fixed."

Corinne's observations were as broken, disrupted, as Kyle's were graceful and assured. "The police didn't believe her, didn't believe there was another car. Finally, a female sheriff took her word for it and flew a helicopter over. That's when they found her car. She wasn't medically insane enough to do something like that."

"Do what? Kill herself?"

"I've been doing research on this since 2000. The investigation is not complete. What she was involved in, I had no idea . . . I googled her. She had incredible security clearance. You know, she was a Fulbright, studying at the European University in Florence. She had access to the diplomatic pouch. She was on the Council on Foreign Relations back before it became this stodgy, respectable . . . She was one of the youngest female members invested. I know the CIA recruits Rhodes scholars. Did they recruit her? It doesn't make any sense.

"She checked in on a Sunday afternoon around one o'clock. I lived in La Jolla, I had rich boyfriends, I liked going to nice hotels. But Lacey shopped at Casual Corner. She was very thrifty. It doesn't make any sense that she was in that hotel."

What Corinne proceeded to tell me didn't make sense to *me*: that Lacey kept calling the front desk to extend her stay. That she could see her own apartment from the balcony of the hotel. That she kept checking her voice mail, even though she made fun of Corinne's obsession with her answering machine.

Then Corinne said, "They found her lying on top of the restaurant awning. I could still see the impression days later when I went to the hotel. Her stupid note was on the table. It's known as the suicide hotel.

"She was meeting someone," Corinne said, her voice huskier

now. "It was clandestine, top secret. That's why she kept checking her voice mail. They found her briefcase. It was empty, except for a life insurance policy. Her briefcase was *never* empty. I went to her apartment a week after, with Anson and Simon. Anson took her laptop right away."

Anson took her laptop. Because it contained classified information? Because of what it would reveal? Before I could ask, she was on to something else, still marshalling the evidence.

"She had read the entire Sunday newspaper cover to cover. And then she went and killed herself? It doesn't make any sense."

Lacey read the entire Sunday paper, cover to cover. Was that in the hope that something would stop her? What was she looking for? Was she like that young man I read about, who left a note on his dresser, saying, "I'm going to walk to the bridge. If one person smiles at me on the way, I will not jump." Tragically, no one smiled at him that day.

Corinne seemed to rest for a moment on the image of her sister. Then she returned to her inventory of clues. "Lacey was very blind. We both are. She wears contacts."

I noticed she was speaking in the present tense.

"The contacts dried out. It drove her crazy. All of her eye stuff was in her apartment. She didn't bring anything to the hotel."

What did that mean? That she didn't intend to stay long? Did the calls, to extend her stay three times, mean she kept changing her mind? Did she finally do it, as Simon was in the air, because she had run out of reasons not to die?

Corinne was silent for a moment. "There was something else," she revealed, as if remembering it for the first time. "There was a chair against the balcony."

"What does that mean?" I asked, gingerly wading in, trying to read the concentric circles of her disorientation and distress.

"I've been on that balcony. You don't need a chair to get over it."

Corinne kept alternating between suspicions of murder and manifest proof that Lacey had killed herself. But the strongest evidence of murder, it turns out, was far more personal. "The suicide note is not in Lacey's writing. It's not her vocabulary."

"It's not?"

"Lacey had a way with words, always did. Her vocabulary was phenomenal. The whole context of the phrases did not sound like Lacey at all. There were misspellings. I didn't delve into it full time because I'd been doing other things. I didn't think about it till four years later. And her car, the accident. I didn't check at the time to see if there was paint on her bumper. Did someone push her off the road? Toxicology reports weren't done. There were so many unanswered questions."

She was quiet for a moment. Then she said softly, "Besides, Lacey only referred to my brother and my mother in the note. Whoever wrote it didn't know her and I were really close again, and her and my dad."

There was something heartbreaking about this moment, about Corinne's almost child-like belief: Lacey could not have written the note, not because it was rambling or ungrammatical, but because it failed to mention *her*.

I sensed the conversation was circling back to its beginnings—Corinne's wish to rescue Lacey. I asked, "How will you find closure? When will your investigation be complete?"

"There are certain people I haven't interviewed. It'll go high up. The evidence is circumstantial. I wouldn't rule out anyone in Lacey's inner circle.

"It could be really dangerous. Not that I think some Special Forces guy is going to come through my door."

Corinne's voice trailed off, intensity giving way to indecision. "There's a 90 percent chance she killed herself. And a 10 percent chance she didn't. I don't know yet."

She was quiet for a moment. "If she did kill herself, she destroyed a family. If someone else killed her, they devastated a family. I don't know if I'll ever know."

33.

An unexpected event devastating a family: that was also something I knew a little about. Like many crises, it began with a phone call. This was three years before I found Lacey's obituary.

"Those red spots in Michael's stomach."

"Who is this?" I asked, rubbing the sleep from my eyes.

"Charlie Frankel, his doctor. I need to reach him."

"It's six o'clock in the morning."

"I know. Those red spots. I had them tested. They're cancer. Cancer of the stomach lining."

Suddenly, I was awake.

I raced to Michael's office to tell him. He was showering after an early morning tennis match. I banged on the door to the little bathroom. He opened it, the water streaming down his face, and smiled at me.

"Charlie Frankel called. You have cancer. Those red spots in your stomach."

He disappeared into the shower again.

After a long moment, he re-emerged.

"Whatever we need to do, we'll do it," he said, and kissed me on the top of the head.

Be angry, I wanted to shout. *Be outraged. Scream. Don't be your usual, reasonable self.*

But he remained reasonable through the grueling process of radiation therapy. He would leave the house at six o'clock every morning for treatment, so he could still drive Isabel to school. He never told her where he was going so early in the morning. And of course we said nothing to Charlotte, who was only two. We told no one, not his family or mine or any of his colleagues. We had seen all these people only months before at Michael's fiftieth birthday party. But Michael didn't want any of them to know.

On the weekends, Michael would put on the pajamas with the seven dwarfs that Charlotte picked out for him and climb into bed and sleep all day. The girls and I would get into the car and drive for hours, up and down the streets of our neighborhood, past the beach, past the playground, past couples strolling along the palisades, dogs tugging at the leash.

Anxiety had patterned my days for as long as I could remember, giving them a beetling texture. Now the undertow of dread swelled exponentially. I was afraid Michael would suffer, that our daughters would suffer, that he might be lost to them forever. I was afraid that, without him, I would be lost again too.

Meanwhile, I was doing little to help him. He didn't want me to go to doctors' appointments, for fear my anxiety would elevate his. I was a mess, frantic and frightened, a kind of whirling dervish, whisking away the clothes he wore to radiation sessions to wash them separately. (I would have burned them if I could.) Forcing him to wash his hands whenever he came home from the clinic. Not wanting to lie near him. Not wanting to kiss him (again). "I'm not radioactive," he would say, but he seemed to glow with the strange effulgence of algae. My fears were ballooning out of control. It was all I could do to remain cheerful and self-contained in front of our children, to hold off the acute despair that loomed, like El Niño in the late summer, threatening to decimate us.

"I want to be one of your friends," Michael once said to me, referring to the women to whom I would bring flowers or a roasted chicken, like I did for Kathy when she was going through chemotherapy. Once she was so exhausted she asked me to lie down beside her in bed. "I haven't been in bed with anyone other than my husband in twenty years!" I joked, as I curled up next to her. But that wasn't strictly true. Maybe that's what I felt guilty about, the dalliance with Anthony. Its unseemliness haunted me to this day. Michael had forgiven me back then, but now, more truly than ever, I was abandoning him. This was the bigger betrayal: letting him soldier on alone. Why could I reach out to Kathy or to Stephanie, who was diagnosed with a brain tumor when her younger son was still an infant? I arranged for someone to come and cook for them every week, freezing meals for the nights Stephanie needed to rest. (My "good works," such as they were, always involved food.) I brought food several times a week to the homeless people near the beach, even after one man scolded me, saying he didn't like soba noodles and would prefer udon next time.

But I was unwilling to nurture Michael, even to notice how vulnerable he seemed. He didn't need me, or so I thought. In photos of him as a little boy, he is standing far from his family, as if, already, he doesn't belong to them. He had gotten away—to Berkeley, the first person in his family to go to college—even taking the family dog, so she could have respite, too. If *anyone* could will himself back to health, it would be Michael.

But I wasn't sure our marriage would ever mend.

34.

I was afraid that Michael might leave me when he got better, if not before. Not just for his sake, but for our kids'. My fears were creating a claustrophobia—a kind of close, tormenting heat—that was stifling my family. Michael's diagnosis was devastating enough.

So I presented myself at the office of the recommended psychopharmacologist, waiting for him to smile or look sympathetic. Instead, he grimaced and gestured to a chair.

I'd scarcely sat down before he asked, "Does it bother you when I move things around?" He was shuffling objects on the little table before me.

Did it bother me?

No. But I had to admit I was somewhat unnerved when he asked me, twice, if I'd ever retraced my route when driving, to make absolutely sure I hadn't driven over anyone. I knew I'd never driven over anyone. But I also knew this man could help me—or at least, proffer pharmaceuticals. So I was willing to consider that the movement of objects on the table bothered me.

I was even willing to answer the ridiculous questions on the questionnaire:

Have you had personal experiences with the supernatural?

Does it often seem that shadows are really people or animals, or that inanimate objects are speaking to you?

Before you were fifteen, did you hurt or threaten someone with a weapon, like a bat, brick, broken bottle, knife, or gun?

The only weapon I ever had was writing. The Irish have a saying, "Most writers are failed talkers." I was a failed talker, wasn't I? I had failed to tell anyone about Joe. I didn't think they would want to know: my parents, embroiled in their furious fights; my brothers, consumed with tales of deadly attacks by apex predators. All those years ago, I wanted someone to ask: Who is this guy? What's he doing? I wanted them to *demand* to know. To awaken when they heard him pounding on the exterior door to my bedroom.

But it was always Joe, not them, growling, "Let me in!"

Night after night, he pulled me down on the bed, tucking his filthy jeans beneath the plush pink blanket; his jeans so tight, you could tell he wasn't wearing underwear. He would reach under my nightgown, his hands rough from the wind, or grab my ponytail, twisting it across my mouth, shoving it into my mouth, so I wouldn't scream.

Do you often feel guilty about the things you want?

About the things you have or haven't done?

35.

Why didn't I reach out to Michael when he needed me? I should have heard him, held him, watched over him while he slept. Instead, I drove our daughters around the neighborhood, noting the houses with real estate signs that said MUST SEE INSIDE. But I hadn't seen inside Michael's trauma. I hadn't helped, or even "hleped."

"We want *you*, not the illness," he implored me. And I knew by "illness," he didn't mean the cancer. He meant whatever it was *I* had. Whatever it was that kept me caged, unable to be myself, unable to be vulnerable. And unable to see how vulnerable he was.

The question of knowledge, of what we allow each other to see, haunted me in the next conversation with Corinne. She resembled her brother most truly in their shared fury at their mother. Corinne fairly hissed when speaking of her.

"My mother was obsessed with Lacey. She was one of those people who live through their children too much. Lacey called her a week before to come up and stay for a few days. My mother didn't do it. Later she thought that, if she had, Lacey wouldn't have killed herself.

"Kyle and I would joke that Mom might do the same thing," Corinne told me. "But we thought probably she'd take pills. She loved to play the victim. Kyle and I used to say, 'Pack your bags, we're going on a guilt trip.'"

After Lorraine's death, Corinne discovered that her mother had tried to kill herself before, just as Lacey had. Her attempts always took place on days of significance to her children: Kyle's birthday. Mother's Day.

"Wasn't she ill?" I asked, remembering something Kyle had said about a disability.

"No. She couldn't open a jar as good."

"I thought he said something about migraines."

"She was addicted to Fioricet. Basically she was a drug addict."

"And she killed herself from the same room?"

"No. The room she wanted was taken. She killed herself from the room next door."

The conversation with Corinne took on its own momentum, hurtling headlong into the dark. I asked questions, throwing them out like gates that she could skid across or avoid altogether, but that would affect her ride.

"Kyle said your mother left an audiocassette. What did it say? Do you remember?"

"'Sorry.'"

"Sorry you don't remember, or sorry you don't want to say?"

"No. The tape said, 'Sorry.' My mother knew it was selfish, but she couldn't go on anymore. She acknowledged it would be horrendously painful. But she didn't want to live without Lacey."

Lacey had been Lorraine's "champion," as Kyle put it. Maybe Lacey sensed her mother's well of need would never be filled. Part of the appeal of Oxford might have been its distance from San Clemente. Having so little money to travel, she might not see her mother again for months. In England, Lacey would be free: to row on the river, to read all afternoon in the rain, to cook for herself, to taste Indian food for the first time. And maybe, for the first time, she would be living life for herself, not trying to make someone else's life worth living. That might have been the greatest benefaction of all.

The tincture of Corinne's grief was very different from her brother's. She seemed more confused, her anger more wrenching, whereas Kyle appeared to have found a measure of peace, perhaps in the sacrament of washing his sister's ring.

He described that moment to me in an email:

After I was notified by the coroner of her suicide, I drove to city hall/coroner's office to collect her personal belongings the police found at the scene. It contained her briefcase, wallet, and other personal effects including the suicide note and her jewelry that she was wearing when she died. The jewelry contained her wedding ring, which she and Simon had commissioned and meant a lot to both of them. It was a beautiful ring that was rather understated, a reflection upon my sister's personality. The ring and a few other items were given a cursory cleaning by the coroner's office. I felt it important to have that ring with me at the airport when I told Simon. When I looked at the ring and other jewelry, I noticed that there was some dried blood on them that had been missed. So, I washed them in my kitchen sink in my apartment and it seemed sort of surreal, almost out of a movie. I was going to ask my girlfriend to do it for me, but upon further reflection—it just seemed like something a brother should take care of personally.

I was struck by the self-consciousness of the moment, as if he was playing a part, performing her last rites. "Something a brother should take care of personally." He had found his role in the family.

I'm not sure either of his sisters ever did.

His message concluded:

I am glad you got a chance to speak with Corinne. I am sure that in the coming weeks, she and I will discuss our own conversations. Perhaps this can be a catalyst for she and I to get on the same page about a few painful things and put them behind us.

I wished I could put to rest Corinne's fear that Lacey had been murdered, although I sensed she might never be at rest. Corinne felt guilty for not having reached out to Lacey or, perhaps, for never having known her at all. Perhaps being known—knowing and being known—is at the root of everybody's longing. It is the deepest gift, and the most elusive, even from ourselves.

Lacey didn't allow anyone, even her husband, to know her. And I wondered: Had I ever really let Michael in? I intended to, telling him on the day we married, "I trust you with more than my life. I trust you with what I want my life to be."

But our wedding video tells a different story. It looks like a slasher film: the videographer forgot to turn off the camera between setups, so the footage lurches violently, and you can hear him panting, like a stalker in pursuit. But the most troubling moment is when the prayer shawl slipped from our shoulders, and I asked the rabbi, "Are we still married?" Even in the midst of the wedding ceremony, I was looking for a way out.

I didn't know that, as Rilke said, lovers can be "solitudes, meeting but never merging." Michael said that was an awkward translation from the German, but it didn't matter. The phenomenon it described was awkward, too. But it was essential: to allow distance, but not isolation. A bit of breathing room, like the holes in the Connemara walls.

Maybe Lacey realized she would never find peace, if she couldn't find it now, with Simon, in her new life. Now she was in a stable marriage, in a great job, in touch with her family.

Now was as good a time as ever to be happy.

Or to go.

36.

But I couldn't move. My fears were paralyzing me. Fears that Michael would come home from the clinic with germs dangerous to our daughters. Fears that he would *never* come home.

So I went back to see the psychopharmacologist, even though it meant retracing my route. Luckily, I *still* hadn't driven over anyone. Maybe, he suggested, with no warmth or empathy, I had OCD. Did I know what that was? He talked at length about the condition, about how I might have inherited it from my father, who was tyrannical, a perfectionist. My aunt washed off the tops of soup cans before she opened them. Maybe she had OCD, too.

As I was talking, the doctor rose up suddenly from his leather chair and strode out the door. A long moment later, he re-appeared with a lengthy article about OCD. "Read this," he said bluntly.

"Where did you go?"

"To get this article."

"But you didn't say anything. It seemed so strange, just to have you get up and walk out of the room when I was in the middle of talking about my husband's illness. I was crying."

"That's the disease talking."

The disease? What about simple manners, empathy?

"You can't tell me it's common just to get up and walk out on someone . . . " I stammered.

He smiled wanly and said nothing.

What ensued was a shouting match. I can't remember how it escalated, but I accused him of being cold and heartless. He said I was sick. "You're going to get yourself into a lot of trouble with that behavior," he warned, as if pronouncing a curse on me.

"And you're going to hurt and alienate a lot of patients with yours."

I charged out of his office and back into the brutish day. I felt abandoned and cursed, and a little ashamed, too. No, I'd never retraced my steps to see if I'd driven over someone. He couldn't convince me that I had.

But I had spent some difficult years washing my hands until they were raw, reaching for a knife from an adjoining table if my cutlery didn't seem clean. I had been damaged, but no, I had never tried to kill myself.

Did I *think* about killing myself?

Doesn't everyone?

PART FIVE

THE PAST IN
ITS PASTNESS

This
Is the process whereby pain of the past in its pastness
May be converted into the future tense
Of joy.

—Robert Penn Warren

37.

We all stay in the world by being connected to other people. That's what I've learned from my research on suicide. It turns out the fewest suicides are in densely packed places: Many more people kill themselves in Alaska or Montana than in New York. At 23.2 suicides per 100,000 people, Wyoming has the highest rate in the country; New York State, at 8 in 100,000, has the lowest. (The national average is 12.4.) Even though more than half of all New Yorkers live alone, Manhattan is among the least likely places to feel lonely. Unless you accidentally smoke some PCP.

Surprisingly, suicide is seasonal, occurring more frequently in the warmer months. More women try to kill themselves, but more men succeed (probably because they have easier access to guns). More American troops commit suicide than die in combat. One in eight American teenagers reports serious suicidal thoughts. According to an article in *The New York Times Magazine,* others at risk include "people with a mental illness like a mood disorder, social isolates and substance abusers, as well as elderly white males, young American Indians, and residents of the Southwest."

I couldn't help but notice one other significant demographic: adults who have suffered abuse as children.

Each year, more than a million people die by their own hand. Suicide claims more lives than homicide and combat combined. Yet, as the article attests, "Our understanding of how suicidal thinking progresses, or how to spot and halt it, is little better now than it was two and a half centuries ago, when we first began to consider suicide a medical rather than philosophical problem and physicians prescribed, to ward it off, buckets of cold water thrown at the head."

But we do know that feeling suicidal is a state that comes and goes. Most of those whose suicides were thwarted share a common reaction in the aftermath. According to Matthew Nock, director of Harvard University's Laboratory for Clinical and Developmental Research, "Virtually all of them say 'I'm glad I didn't die.'"

And most never try to kill themselves again.

But Lacey had. Perhaps the final key to understanding her was Simon, her husband, happily ensconced in England with his new wife.

But what would I ask him? "So, your wife killed herself on the day you were flying over to begin your life together. Do you know why?"

I'd read about a woman who committed suicide, whose husband found her body. "Her eyes were open," he reported. "The look was of wonder, not horror." I remembered that Simon hadn't seen Lacey at the end. What was the last thing she thought before she went out of the world? And what was his world like, without her in it?

But by now Simon had moved on, hadn't he? Would he want some stranger to contact him? To talk about his first wife, his *late* wife, who hadn't died of cancer, like my freshman roommate, going reluctantly out of the world, reaching back to the living. Lacey Cooper-Reynolds had *fled*.

But I needn't have been so cautious in approaching Simon, as I soon discovered. He sounded resoundingly stable, even remote.

From the first, he seemed to approach the subject as if it were a clinical investigation.

"The Rhodes Scholarship attracts people who are predisposed to be overachievers," he said when we launched in. "Or do they push themselves in situations where, even if they feel uncomfortable, they are driven to succeed? Sometimes 'drive' can be seen as a means of taking advantage of opportunities and achieving. The question is, 'Are they predisposed to that sort of problem or does the Rhodes Scholarship . . . '"

He was quiet for a moment. Then he resumed, "The Rhodes Scholarship epitomizes the problem of drive."

I was silent. He was, as he said early in the conversation, a "social scientist." But he had also been Lacey's husband. Where was that person now?

"Lacey was very strongly driven," he continued. "Whether that was due to family or genetics, I don't think any of us will ever know. She was a classic overachiever, an extreme version of an overachieving personality."

Then he drew back the curtain to reveal something truly intimate. "I saw that in a situation that was completely nonacademic. I like to play squash. She wanted to play me in squash, she wasn't very good, and it was getting really ugly on the squash court. She accused me of playing down to her, and she was right. But if I did play as well as I could, we would barely have had a game. Naturally, I slowed down a bit."

Suddenly, he sounded like a harried husband, well meaning but confounded; it was a tone I knew well.

"Lacey did not like me to adjust my game to reflect her weakness, her amateur . . . " Here his voice trailed off. "She couldn't bear to lose."

All at once, he fell silent, and I listened to the line grow still. I wasn't sure what to say. Then, finally: "I hear you were her moral tutor."

He laughed. "It's an archaic thing, not like an academic

supervisor. If someone has financial problems, personal problems, you're meant to take some responsibility. The term itself is a bit ludicrous really."

"And you two fell in love?"

"It all happened pretty quickly. Honestly, I forget the exact timing."

"Was it unusual for someone to fall in love with a tutor?"

"It was an issue because it was unusual. I told my head of department about it very promptly. 'This is what's happening. I'm not her academic supervisor.'"

I asked if he ever sensed any problems while supervising Lacey in a tutorial role.

"She didn't have problems," he said, almost defensively. Then, "She ceased being my moral tutee." Was he uncomfortable because it was so sad, or because it was ancient history?

"We met when Lacey was in the last year of her MPhil in international relations. She decided to stay on and do the DPhil. Her doctorate," he said, providing the name of the equivalent American degree. "I had only seen the really confident, exuberant side of Lacey, with the exception of that squash game and a few discussions about her supervisor. She had the normal anxiety about how she would do on her final exams. She was highly competent, capable. Anyone you'd tell, they'd say this was the last person in the world this would happen to. I think she did that strategically.

"It was really only after that, some of the deeper anxieties started to creep out. The PhD turned out to be quite a difficult, even traumatic, thing for her.

"She didn't believe it was good enough. I couldn't help her, but she felt the whole thing was in danger of collapse."

"And was it?"

"She'd give her supervisor a chapter and he'd say, 'Great job. I look forward to the next one.' But Lacey thought Rick wasn't smart enough to see the weaknesses in it. It was frustrating."

Suddenly it hit me; her advisor, whom Simon called "Rick,"

was the Frederick Malcolmson who provided the foreword to her book. He made a case for how pertinent, even important, her discoveries were, but what was most compelling was his shock at her demise. ("When the terrible news came that she had taken her own life, it was so difficult to credit. Someone less likely to have done so would be difficult to imagine.") Now it appeared she thought he wasn't very smart. Because he admired her work? Or because he was oblivious to her despair?

"Why didn't she take a job in academia, like you?" It was a question I had always wanted to ask.

"She probably thought she could make a lot of money. She had all these skills. Her family had chronic financial problems. They were kicked out of all these rental properties after her dad left."

"So she felt the need to be financially independent?"

"It was fine for me to be on an academic salary, a pittance." There was nothing self-pitying in his voice. "I was glad she did not go for it. She felt so anxious over the PhD. I thought her skills were very suited to the business world."

Did Lacey worry that Simon didn't think she was smart enough? Was she a prisoner of his expectations, too, imagined or otherwise?

I remembered that Nabokov wrote about a gorilla who learned to draw. The first picture the animal made was of the bars of his cage. Maybe we are all imprisoned, most especially by other people's perceptions—misperceptions—of us.

And in the breach between who you are and the *image* of you, so much can be lost.

Suddenly, Simon's voice flooded with emotion, as if he could sense the fear spiraling up Lacey's spine. "At first, no one saw Lacey's car crash as a cry for help. It was interpreted as an accident. But a colleague of mine said he knew someone who had gotten hit on the head and killed himself a week later. Neurological damage. It was tempting to believe it had a simple, exogenous cause."

I marveled that he used words like "exogenous" so casually.

His eloquence measured the distance between Oxford and the beach town where Lacey was born, between the world she ascended to and the world she struggled to escape.

"After her death, I went to see a lot of therapists to talk about it. Obviously, it was a suicide attempt. Oh God, of course it was!"

A cry for help.

It was the first time I heard an expression of despair, as if the horror of the realization was still fresh.

38.

I thought of the people in my life who had reached out to me, whose pleas I had ignored, like the girl in the yellow sweater. More than fifteen years later, Simon's words seem to summon her again.

In my early thirties, before I had children, I received a very small grant from the American Film Institute to make a very small film. I had never held a movie camera before, but all those years at the Taper, helping playwrights "fix" their plays, had whetted my appetite. I wanted to make something of my own.

My film was about a young woman who got caught up in something she couldn't control. Her name was Jill, and her beau's name was Jack, and I called the movie *Tumbling After*. It was all very obvious. Or rather, it was all ridiculously autobiographical, the way many first films are. I cast a young actress who looked like a much more beautiful version of me, and she fell in love with the actor playing Jack, who was a heroin addict, and they insisted on sleeping over in the set, a derelict apartment, so they could get a better "feel" for their characters (and each other).

It was Michael's idea to show the movie at my old high school, to return to the world by the water from which I fled. I ended up screening the film in the cafeteria where Joe used to show up, tapping on the window, gesturing to me. I would climb into his car and we would drive across the street to a meadow, carpeted with white clover and cornflower and lamb's ear. It was a beautiful place, almost balmy, with bees the size of hummingbirds, and there was never anyone there but us.

Joe would nibble my shoulder, somewhere he thought no one would notice, even as I reached for my book bag in the backseat.

"Jessie! Put that shit away! I didn't come up here to have you read a book."

"Why *did* you come?"

"You told me you had lunch at 11:45."

"And I'm supposed to be eating lunch. I could get in trouble."

He laughed and pulled me in closer. "Yeah, right. As if anybody cares."

Now, as the film unspooled, I saw a girl in the front row, fourteen or fifteen years old, tensing, leaning forward when Jill asks Jack's mother for help. I had noticed her earlier, the dirty collar of her shirt, the yellow sweater with a tear in it, from a nail maybe, or a careless friend.

"How did you do it?" she asked me when the lights came up.

I wasn't sure what she meant. How did I make the movie? Or how did I engineer my escape?

After the screening, I went to the faculty room with Mr. Gottshalk, the jovial music teacher. I had never been in the teachers' lounge before, yet it felt as frozen as a museum diorama, the chipped Formica tables, the yellowed tea bags, the newspapers no one finds time to read. Many of the teachers seemed happy to see me and asked about life in Los Angeles. Mrs. Ackerman remembered an essay I wrote in fourth grade, saying she still showed it to her students. Mrs. Kern remembered rebuking me for talking in class.

"Who is the girl in the yellow sweater?" I blurted out.

"She's a tenth grader," Mr. Gottshalk told me. "She lives with her father and her grandparents. Her mother's gone."

"Gone?"

"She's moved to Hawaii, I think. She has other kids now."

Why would a mother leave her child behind?

"What does the father do?" I asked Mr. Gottshalk, awkwardly, as he insisted that I call him "Bob." I called him "Mr. Bob."

"He works around the house, I think. I don't know. We never see him. The grandmother comes to school sometimes. Not a lot."

"Is someone hurting her?"

"The grandmother?"

"No, the girl. She doesn't look happy."

He stared down at his plate.

"Is somebody hurting her?" I asked again, but what I really wanted to know was: Is anyone reaching out to her?

These were the same people who let Joe take me across the street to the meadow to molest me. The same people who waved as I walked out, those valedictory waves, as if we were at a Fourth of July party or a parade.

I was much further out than you thought
And not waving but drowning.

That was from a Stevie Smith poem I loved when I was young.

Help her, I wanted to shout, louder than the banging on the window when Joe came to school, louder than his longing, louder than my father's tirades when we made too much noise in the house or something broke.

Please help.

Help the girl in the yellow sweater.

Help the girl in my movie.

Help me.

39.

"She told me she just wanted to go to the top of Mulholland," Simon was saying. "She'd been working all night; she'd not been up to the top to see the city lights. She said a car came along and caused her to veer off the road. In retrospect, she just made that up."

He took a breath. "The air bags deployed. She found herself alive after being unconscious for an hour or so."

Then another breath.

"Crawled back up."

Here he stopped, as if seeing her in her confusion, bruised and bleeding. Then I remembered: He never saw her injured. Kyle and Corinne were the ones who tended to her.

"It was a week before I was to arrive in L.A. I was in the middle of exams. I could have gotten out of it. She insisted I stick with my plan. She kept insisting she was absolutely fine."

Earlier his phrases were measured, balanced. He had an academician's ability to see both sides. Now he was *enacting* both sides, and his words were fractured, urgent, as if he could still hear her arguments in his head.

"I kept insisting, 'I've got to come over.' She got a bit angry. 'I'm just bruised. Please don't come.' She couldn't bear to face me.

I was the trigger, in the decision to kill herself and to kill herself when she did, because I was arriving. Failing me. She couldn't face me."

Simon sounded as bewildered as he was self-assured when our conversation began. It had been late afternoon, he had seemed poised, relaxed, confident, but vigilant. Now it was evening, and he sounded despondent, disoriented.

"It was difficult to deal with. It was not my fault. The cause was in part me. It was the Chatsworth job, and now she was in a marriage, which was for life. It upped the stakes."

I knew what he meant. The "stakes" are very high if you take marriage seriously. Michael did; *so* seriously, he wanted us to see a marriage counselor even before we were married. At the time, I accused him of wanting out of the relationship.

"I don't want out," he said. "I want in."

But "in" was where Joe had been, and where I feared to let anyone venture. "In" was where I rarely went myself.

All these years later, I was still trying to explain the source of my phobias through genetics and the trauma with Joe. But Michael didn't "buy it," and he wouldn't let it go. Every argument brought us back to this central rupture: my fear and his frustration. And every time, our bond lapsed further into loss.

It had been three years since his last radiation treatment, but the wound of my absence was still raw. Almost any topic of conversation could further inflame it, even—perhaps especially—if it concerned my mom.

"I told my mother that Isabel has really good radar," I said as I was emptying the dishwasher. He was reading about the Lakers, or trying to read. "But my mom said that doesn't always work. You can't always count on your instincts or whatever. To keep you safe."

Michael didn't look up. "I think she's right. I think you can't control things. You can't control *anything*."

"You can be vigilant and try to make things happen, the things you know are right."

"That's just an illusion. We have no control over anything. It's all a giant leap of faith."

"That's bullshit!" I cried, more forcefully than I meant to. The clean utensils clattered to the floor.

"Mommy, are you okay?" Charlotte called from the next room. I had forgotten she was there, playing with her plastic animals.

I turned to Michael. "See? That's what my mother never did. She never checked in to say, 'Are you alright? Is something troubling you?'"

"You've got to let that go already. Maybe she knew, and maybe she didn't."

"How could she not know? He was coming to their house at night!"

"Is someone coming, Mommy?" Charlotte asked.

"Shhh," Michael hissed. "Let's not talk about it now."

"Let's not talk about it *ever* is what you really mean."

"I'm not your mother. Don't confuse me with her."

"But you're taking her side against me. I thought you were on *my* team."

"I happen to think she's right."

"She never liked you anyway!"

"Well, she's not right about *everything*."

"That isn't funny."

He put down his cup. "It's not funny. It's sad. How many kids aren't allowed to eat takeout because hot food shouldn't be put in plastic?"

"But that's true."

"It doesn't matter."

"It matters to me."

"No, the *plastic* doesn't matter. What matters is depriving them, making them feel unsafe. Little things aren't toxic. M&M's."

"But you know those bowls in restaurants by the hostess desk? You can't imagine the traces of urine on those peanuts!"

"Who has peanuts?" Charlotte asked.

"Charlotte, go upstairs," Michael growled. "I want to talk to Mommy."

"You're shouting!" She ran off, tearily.

Now Michael was really upset. "I don't want to live like this. All these fears! It makes me sick."

"You didn't get cancer because of me."

"No. But you were worthless. You couldn't help me. You were so terrified."

"I was afraid you were going to die."

"You were afraid I would bring germs into the house!"

"You said we'd be remiss if we didn't use your illness to get closer."

"But we didn't. Let's be honest. We're not. I don't want to live this way anymore, where everything's toxic. *I'm* toxic."

He threw down the newspaper.

"Michael . . . "

"I'm not doing this anymore. I don't give a shit that your mother never liked me! You're just like her. Nothing's ever good enough. I'm not some consolation prize."

He got up suddenly, tripping over the dog, who was perpetually poised beneath the kitchen table. "I want out!"

40.

❦

"It was not obvious that things were deteriorating," Simon told me, his voice grave. "Lacey was incredibly capable at managing other people's perceptions. That was her primary skill set. Like a lot of kids with alcoholic parents—her father was—her social skills were highly developed. She said she had the 'gift of gab.' She saw it as a means by which she could fool the world."

"Did she ever say she was depressed?"

"Certainly the signs were there. She clearly did not want to talk about it. She just walked away. That wasn't a conversation we could have."

"Could she say those things to anyone?"

"Not to me, not to her family, not to her mother, who was completely dependent on her and useless. You know, it's a strong character trait of kids who are children of alcoholics; they're very perceptive. That's how they survive. Picking up on small changes in behavior."

His voice trailed off again.

"I didn't think of myself as good at that sort of thing. We would joke about how I was the typical male, fairly sunny, life was pretty easy, no serious hardships. I was the pupil when it came to social skills, psychology. I didn't think I had very much to offer. I hadn't been through what she'd been through. Obviously, she leant on me in other ways."

His use of the English version of "leaned" was poignant, archaic.

"I could help her," he said, as if trying to be brave, in the way a child does. In fact, he seemed uncertain, even now, of what he might have done. "I just felt those kinds of conversations became frustrating. I would try to bolster her confidence and it wouldn't work."

"Did she ever consult a therapist?"

"Her stepmother, Jackie, thought she should see someone. Lacey just laughed. 'That's for weak people,' she would say. 'It's not something I need.'"

His voice was hushed and sorrowful. Where initially he had seemed authoritative, he was pensive, piecing together a narrative, seeing the picture emerge even as he missed it then. "I was pretty ignorant. I had little experience of depression. It was all fairly hypothetical to me. And there was much that she hid from me. She maintained the impression of someone who was completely capable, strong."

Could he tell that she was struggling?

"If we got to a restaurant and got a bad table, she would complain. She would do it all the time, in a way that was even a bit embarrassing. She was capable of being quite confrontational, in a charming way. She could pull it off."

He was silent. I jumped in, describing the three photos I had of Lacey: one of her as a child with Kyle, one on her wedding day, and one with her mother, Lorraine. In that last photo, Lacey's face was close to the camera, full and confident, and I could feel her italicized charm. But in her wedding photo, she looked gaunt.

"Had she been losing weight?"

"The last time I saw her alive, April 1995, during Easter vacation, she'd lost a lot of weight. I said, 'I can cook for you. You're working too hard.' She said, 'I've got a long way to go in terms of losing weight.' I didn't understand. 'All those sad, L.A. X-ray types. You don't think like that.' She just shrugged. I didn't really register that at the time. No doubt she'd lost her appetite. A classic sign of depression. I read it in books after she died."

41.

For weeks after our fight, Michael and I circled each other warily. When our *ketubah* fell off the wall during an earthquake, neither of us bothered to hang it back up. But we had spent months writing those vows:

Together we shall be
Celebrant of each other's joy
Minister to each other's sorrow
Midwife to each other's hopes
Confidant to each other's fears
Sentry to each other's solitude
Companion to each other's best self
Guardian of our children's independence and self-respect.

It was Michael who added the last line about our children. It was his idea to place them there with us.

Now we had fallen away from those ideals, even from the will to be civil. Every snore was a call to battle; every unwashed dish, a dare. One day we argued so loudly about which of us would lift the dog over the doggy gate that she finally leapt over the barrier herself.

Why, when Charlotte was crying, would the dog try to console her by bringing her a toy? Didn't she know she had once been wild, once been a wolf?

But wolves are very kind to each other, someone told me. Maybe they feel kinship, loyalty, even where we do not. Sometimes, at the park, pushing Charlotte on the swing, I would let Emma off her leash, even though you weren't supposed to. Why did she never want to run away? Other dogs were escape artists, but ours craved our company. Why did she want to be so close? Why would she calibrate the distance between us, when I was folding laundry or washing a pot, to see if she could settle even closer, on my feet? I had trouble with "boundaries," but she did not. She knew no boundaries. She felt only love.

"Emma the dilemma," a friend called her, perhaps unfairly, but the dilemma she posed was real: how to love unconditionally, to give oneself fully.

Somehow she could do it.

I could not.

As Michael recovered from cancer, he began to sleep less and bake more. He'd always believed every birthday cake should be made from scratch; so, too, every pancake. Now he resolved to teach our daughters to cook. When we were first engaged, I tried to make him pasta, and he said it tasted like electrical wire. (When had he ever tasted *that*?) So I long ago ceded the kitchen to him, and Isabel once told a friend's mother that I didn't cook because I wasn't tall enough to reach the stove.

MAKE YOURSELF BIGGER, it said on a sign near our house, where you can hike into the Santa Monica Mountains. A mountain lion had been spotted there. I loved that, the wildness, the closeness of its presence, but it was easy to love that proximity from behind a fence. I hadn't made myself bigger in the face of Michael's illness. It was a bear that had nearly devoured us. But now, slowly, I began to take risks, every day, my own kind of aversion therapy, using a dirty fork in a restaurant, or retrieving something from the floor without washing my hands. I didn't flinch if a stranger leaned in too close or showered me with spittle. And I promised not to balk if, when Michael felt stronger, we decided to travel again, even if my seatmate was wearing a hazmat suit.

But I could not help feeling shame at how I had treated him. Was I like my mother? I had abandoned him when he needed me most. It was one thing to yield the kitchen to him, given that I thought dinner was done when the smoke alarm sounded. I had no "simmer," he would say, no sense of moderation, but I would try. That was one of the things I had learned from Lacey: not to conceal one's challenges, but not to "catastrophize" them, either. To address each problem as squarely, rationally, as possible (or, at least, at a lower volume). My daughters helped by calling me "less stress Jess."

42.

⤜

"Lacey fled as fast and as far as possible from one hard-earned honor to the next, hoping this would somehow change the way she felt," according to her obituary. She was always running, but she could not escape the pressure of her new job. "You know, other people did not make it through Chatsworth," Simon told me, then corrected himself. "That's the wrong term. There were other people who found that Chatsworth wasn't right for them, like Esther. She was a Fulbright. Eventually she realized that going to Chatsworth was the worst decision she ever made. She quit."

"Why didn't Lacey do that?"

"She couldn't admit failure. Esther is a stronger person, being able to recognize when something isn't making you happy. Lacey had all sorts of other options, but she didn't want to fail in front of me and other high-achieving friends. She was surrounded by a community of overachievers. That made it all the more impossible to exit from."

He came to a stop. I jumped in, saying people kept telling me Lacey wasn't very good at math. He readily agreed.

"At the end of her stay at USC, they had to give her some

sort of remedial exam to make sure she got her degree, so she wouldn't fail. She'd have had to give up her Rhodes."

"Is that why she struggled at Chatworth, because of her math skills?"

"Chatsworth did not employ her because of her math skills. They did not need everyone to have the same strengths. A lot of people were saying she was actually doing very well."

Here, again, he took a long breath. Then, without warning, he was speaking in Lacey's voice.

"'I'm useless at it; they've given me a soft project, a less quantitative project, pro bono.'"

Before I could respond, a different voice interjected: the voice of Chatsworth & Company. "'We won't put her on a heavy project. We'll allow her to build her confidence.'"

"Was Lacey unhappy with her assignment?"

"It reinforced her perception that she was qualitatively weak. That's how she looked at things, but not how most people would."

I ventured that it was a bit like wanting to play a good squash player right off. He agreed.

"So many of her friends, people she respected, had gone to Chatsworth. It was almost a next step on from a Rhodes Scholarship, for a lot of Americans in particular. Failure there would prove the whole thing was a house of cards."

Lacey. Esther. What about Risa? A trio of talented women, plagued by self-doubt.

"I recall Risa telling me she'd had a phone conversation with Lacey. Lacey's friends had all these anxieties, and she would help them understand their problems. She understood people very well; she could get them to talk. Risa had been thinking in fairly grim terms: she worked ridiculous hours, both at Oxford and at Chatsworth. She confided in Lacey, and Lacey comforted her."

"Is that why Risa never wanted to talk with me?"

"Those are sort of deep waters," Simon allowed, and I marveled at his powers of discretion. Was he just too decent, too buoyant, to take the measure of his wife's despair? "Anson told me Risa is more relaxed now. She's taken time off. Possibly it was a bit too close to the bone for Risa."

Possibly.

Like Corinne, Simon noted that Chatsworth had discontinued the mini-MBA program Lacey once struggled to complete. But I wondered if the company's biggest concession was an intriguing passage in their mission statement:

> We go to great lengths to help the people we hire to succeed. We are passionate about mentoring the people who work at Chatsworth. Those who work here work among people united by their values and an atmosphere of trust, caring, respect, support and interdependence.

The emphasis on connection, on interdependence. Maybe that was Lacey's legacy.

In the background, I could hear the voices of Simon's young children, his five-year-old son and eight-year-old daughter. Later he revealed that he'd yet to tell them about Lacey, although he expected to, at some point.

"Simon," he said quietly.

Was that the name of his son?

"That was the grief counselor."

Only in a farce by Feydeau or Michael Frayn would the grief counselor and the widower have the same name. I didn't say this, as Simon's thoughts had gained a kind of momentum. His children's voices had heartened him.

"Sy spent a lot of time with me. He was a good guy. An ex-marine/priest/troubleshooter. I would talk to anyone at the time, but he was helping in a practical way."

"He was sent by Chatsworth?"

"Yes. It was a very self-interested action on their part. Here was someone freely available, without charge. 'If you need something, Sy will fix it up.' It was disaster management on their part. Look, Chatsworth did all they could. They paid expenses, dispatched Sy, though he quickly fled the scene once it became obvious no one was going to sue. No one was going to cause them any problems."

"What kind of problems could they cause?"

"They were concerned about how this would go over in the press. Its effect on corporate morale, which, in the L.A. office, wasn't very good. There were others there who had all these anxieties."

I remembered Kyle's description: *other people who might have jumped.*

"They created a scholarship for her at USC," Simon told me cheerily. "They even sponsored Lacey's funeral. And they gave Anson quite a lot of time off. Chatsworth did not walk away from it. But they had a clear interest in preventing trouble being made about what kind of work hours were expected, what kind of mentoring they were providing for young people. It could have been bad news for them."

Simon relayed all this quite genially. He hadn't made himself a victim. It was impossible to say anyone was at fault. Sure, it was damage control, but he wasn't blaming Chatsworth. Besides, what difference would it make at this late date?

When Nelson Mandela was released from prison after twenty-seven years—18 of them spent on Robben Island, where he was routinely thrown into solitary confinement for the slightest infraction and endured hard labor in the blistering sun—he immediately forgave his captors. His supporters were stunned. "I knew if I didn't leave my bitterness and hatred behind, I'd still be in prison," he said later. His enemies had taken so much from him. He wouldn't give them any more of his time.

43.

Someone once said there are only two kinds of luggage, "carry-on" and "lost." But survivors know a third kind, the burden one shoulders, unsuspected. We balance its weight on our hip like a baby, tending to it like a phantom limb.

When do we finally put down that burden? How much time will we forfeit before we set ourselves free? Sometimes liberation presents itself serendipitously, on the way to the shoe store or the book mart. We don't always see the EXIT sign.

A few years before I met Michael, I went to Lloyd Harbor to visit my parents, but I spent most of the time holed up in my room. Carson McCullers said, "I must go home periodically to renew my sense of horror." But the most awful thing was the black mold that had overtaken my closet, flocking the walls like wallpaper and tarring the floor. The smell was overpowering, so when my mother invited me to go for a drive, I readily agreed. Where were we going? She would not say.

Then we pulled into the mouth of the harbor, home of the Orlando School of Ballet. Only the dilapidated Victorian, which had housed the dancers and studios, was gone, burned to the ground. In its place was a charred and lurching hulk.

"Oh my God!" I gasped.

"I know," my mother said evenly. "Pretty dramatic, huh?"

"What about Betty and Vinnie?"

"Betty's dead. But not in the fire. Though it destroyed all those cats. And the costumes. Well, you remember that house. It's all gone now."

"And Vinnie?"

"He lives across the street, above the deli. With his new wife. And his two sons."

"He has kids?"

"Stepkids. Can you believe he remarried?"

I couldn't believe he had married in the first place, but it was a different time back then. Suddenly, there was a knock on the window of my mother's Subaru. It was Chris, another of the dancers from that time. He'd always seemed pretty benign, a bit embarrassed to be seen in tights. What he really wanted to do was work with wood.

I rolled down the window. "Hey, Chris, how are you?"

"Jessie! How are you?"

"Good. How is everything?" The question seemed moronic, given the skeletal structure just in front of us.

"Good. Everything's good."

"Good," I said, and because the inane exchange threatened to go on like this forever, I blurted out, "Is Vinnie around?"

"Yeah, I think he's upstairs."

"I'd like to see him. Can you ask him to come down?"

"Why?"

"I want to talk to him."

"Nah," Chris said, his voice ever genial. "He doesn't want to come down right now. He's having dinner with his family."

I thought of Vinnie at the dinner table, insulated by the lively smells of the deli. What would have happened, if he had come down? If I had confronted him, all these years later, about the violence in that attic bedroom? Did his new wife know what had happened on his watch?

Years before, Vinnie had choreographed a *pas de deux* for Joe and me to music by Brahms. Whenever I hear its insinuating oboe, I still grow afraid. For the dance was a re-enactment of the violence between us: Joe pretending to beat me. And me—on pointe shoes—pretending to dodge his blows.

Dance, I always thought, had ardor and amplitude. But this was meaningless pointillism, disconnectedness. And my parents sat in the audience and watched, my father peering through his rolled-up program like a periscope. Didn't they wonder what it meant?

I thought of all those rehearsals, the late-night dinners, cats climbing over the candles. All the dancers, smoking on the steps. All those afternoons in the stifling attic. All those terrible lies.

Now here I was, at the scene of the crime, but the crime scene had gone missing. In its place was a scarred shell, hideous and marred. This violent place had become outwardly all that it had always been in my mind. Maybe it would no longer haunt my dreams. If a dungeon has been blown open, the sky streaming through its broken portals, maybe its prisoners can finally exit, bruised and blinking, into the sun. Maybe there would be no need, anymore, to keep these secrets.

Maybe there never was.

So I told my mother what happened there, how Joe had beaten me when I wouldn't have sex with him. That's why I wanted to leave school, to go to Paris. Did she remember the Pasquiers? She never turned to look at me as I spoke, never reached over to touch me. Her eyes were fixed on the fishing boats, coming home from a late-day run. I thought she might want to hug me—we weren't wearing our seat belts—or say "I'm so sorry" or "I wish I had known" or "I should have known" or "What can I do now?"

Instead, she said, after a long moment, "You were so secretive. You must not have wanted us to know."

* * *

Twenty years later, my mother and I were sitting in Charlotte's bedroom, staring at the bed—or rather, at the wooden bed frame that had arrived that morning. The mattress seemed to float within it like a raft. Charlotte had to catapult herself off the bed or risk falling into the open space between the mattress and the frame. My mother was disgusted. How hard would it be to find the right-size mattress? I told her I had ordered one. It was on its way.

I don't know if it was the feeling of being judged that unleashed my fury, or being in the small bedroom together, or the heat. Or maybe it was rage at never confronting her about what happened in my own bedroom all those years ago, letting it insulate me like a filthy blanket on a freshly made bed.

"Why did you let it happen?"

"What?"

"With Joe. Do you know how miserable it's made me?"

"I didn't know it was happening."

"How is that possible? He was coming to my room at night!"

"You never told us."

"I didn't know what to say."

"And you loved dancing. You always wanted to go there. To Vinnie's."

That's true. I did love dancing, but not the way Isabel loves it, using it to heal something she does not understand.

I thought back to that conversation in front of the ruined ballet school, when my mother said I must not have wanted them to know. "Now that you know, can you say you're sorry or something?"

"I can *say* I'm sorry, but it won't mean anything. I didn't know."

"But can you say you're sorry that someone you love, your only daughter, has suffered?"

"I can *say* I'm sorry. But it won't *mean* anything."

"Why can't you just acknowledge what happened, what it meant to *me*?"

"How do you know it's not happening, right now, to Isabel?"

What? I marveled that she could say her granddaughter's name in such a context. It seemed as sudden, as violent, as a slap.

"It could be happening right now to Isabel," my mother insisted.

"It's not," I said simply. "I know."

She regarded me calmly, dry eyed, as if I was part of an especially lively book club, as if my pain had nothing to do with her.

"Don't you see how much I've struggled? Sometimes I can't even leave my house."

"Look. Whatever I say, it won't be enough for you," my mother ventured. "I know that. It never was."

"You don't know me at all."

"Oh, I know you. I know exactly who you are. You're dangerous. And cruel." She thought for a moment. "Besides, back then we didn't know a lot about these things."

What *things?* I wondered. She hadn't even acknowledged something had happened, but now she was making reference to it by its absence. How strange was that? Suddenly, we were having an abstract argument about meaning and existence in Charlotte's bedroom, when all I wanted was an apology, an embrace. All I wanted was to hear her say, "I'm sorry, Jess. I love you." And even, "I believe you. I really do. It's just that, when you told me what happened, I didn't know what to do about it." Or maybe: "I was so unhappy. All I wanted was my life with Jan."

But she did not say any of this, as I sat there sobbing. She couldn't. She was a wizened old woman, lively and charming, but she was *done.* She never wanted to excavate other people's feelings, to examine motive, to understand behavior. She certainly wouldn't want to do that now. My mother had a great appreciation for the fineness of a stripe on a vintage linen, but she could never see beyond the onyx surface of my despair. The "bigger picture" was impenetrable to her gaze, and it always had been. She didn't want to see it. And she never would.

I had to stop asking for something she could never give, and maybe I didn't need it anymore. It wasn't going to take away my sorrow. Only I could do that; I knew that now. If she thought I was dangerous and cruel—so powerful—maybe I was strong enough to do this: to let go of my rage. To acknowledge, to accept, my mother's limitations: that she would defend herself instead of defending me.

I had to let go: of my mother and Joe and Vinnie. They needed to fly from me, like cows in a tornado, immovable objects that are suddenly aloft. I didn't need to carry them anymore, to look back, to find justification. I didn't need to look forward, either. I could just be. "You are searching for something you haven't lost," it says in the Talmud. Maybe I wasn't as broken as I thought, as fragile or flawed. Yes, I had been lost: foundering and desperate and self-destructive. But I had also been chosen. I had also been found.

44.

Now I no longer ended every therapy session with the question: "Why didn't I tell anyone?" And my shrink (a nice one this time) no longer had to respond: "There was no one to tell." I knew that part of the recovery from any trauma is the telling of it, knowing you will *survive* the telling of it. The telling can launch you on the path to peace.

The telling allows you to see the suffering of others. I thought of that as I listened to Simon describe Lacey's parents, her "broken" home.

"I used to blame them," he said, "but Kyle grew up in the same situation. He turned out fine. Although Lacey protected him a lot; she took on the parenting burdens. She provided a stable anchor for him."

He took a breath.

"I still feel quite close to him. He was the one who went through a similar experience to mine."

I asked him to clarify something he said earlier, about suicides who leave "a long, explanatory note." Didn't Lacey leave some kind of message? I remembered that Kyle had mentioned a suicide note.

"Yes, it was four or five lines in cramped, small writing. I used to know it by heart. 'I'm so sorry. I just can't do this anymore. The horror.'"

"'The horror?'"

"I have no idea what it means. 'I love Simon. I love Kyle.'" He was quoting it to me now.

"What was 'the horror?'"

"Chatsworth? Fear of failing? Going back to her mother? Now she was only an hour and a half away. Her mother was closing in."

"Her mother was 'the horror?'"

"It was pretty disjointed. Not the best thing Lacey ever wrote."

Then, tellingly, he could not remember what he did with it. It was his first moment of ringing unclarity.

"I threw it away. Or I think Kyle and I burned it. I can't recall. I may have given it to her mum."

I remembered that Simon stayed in L.A. for a year and a half after Lacey's death. To do what? Get his career on track? Comfort Lacey's family?

"Kyle taught me to Rollerblade." He was quiet for a moment. "You know, I think about Kyle, in a way, more than Lacey. Somehow your psyche heals."

Your psyche heals, but only if you let it. You can't keep gnawing at things, like a dog with a stick. Sometimes Emma, our dog, would mutter, restless on the rug: Was she having a nightmare? If a dog can cry out, when she has known only love, it is only human that we would suffer. That is how we grow.

But habitual gloom is different from suffering. It has an expansive treachery, like mold. The mold in my childhood bedroom had ruined everything: high school yearbooks and pointe shoes and all my Madame Alexander dolls. The only survivor was Louisa May Alcott's Jo. I'd always liked her best, anyway: She was a writer. She wanted a bigger life. She suspected that Marmie was selling her a bill of goods. But if *Little Women* taught me anything, it was that one could wrestle free of her circumstances. I couldn't blame my "mother issues" on Louisa May Alcott. I couldn't blame them on anyone.

Lacey had called her mother "the horror," never suspecting that her mother would kill herself, and at the same hotel, or that they would be buried near each other in the San Clemente dirt. They had put her mother far enough away not to annoy her, Kyle had said, as if Lacey's mother, more than anything, had kept her from happiness.

My mother wasn't a "horror;" she never abandoned us or burned us with cigarettes. She had her books and her dog and her own snarling sense of loss. She had a mother who was demanding and frequently indisposed, perpetually discontented. I'm not sure she valued her daughter any more than my mother did me. As a child, my mother went to her art classes, and read her novels, and cared for Pepper, her cocker spaniel, and listened for her sickly mother on the stairs. To be a mother was to be undisturbed and to be disgruntled. To be a mother was to be alone.

"Children begin by loving their parents," Oscar Wilde wrote. "As they grow older they judge them; sometimes they forgive them." Maybe I could forgive her now. Not for her sake, but for mine, for my children. Not because she deserved it, but because we do. "To forgive," means "to give again" or "to give as in the past," but I wanted to give as I had never given before. To give wholly, freely, without hesitation. To love fearlessly, as I had longed to all my life.

I would have to move on, or remain trapped forever in my anger, distant from my children, from Michael, unable to hold them. Unable to see that the laughter at the dinner table, the snuggling in bed, was part of a larger force—of goodness or redemption—that I was privileged to be part of. That was ready to be savored, right now.

"You will never be a whole person, if you can't acknowledge what happened to me," I'd told my mother, softly, that day in Charlotte's bedroom. I didn't mean it as condemnation. It was the saddest thing I'd ever said. You will never be whole, if you can't feel tenderness or sorrow or compassion.

You will never be a whole person.

But I will.

45.

Several weeks later, I noticed that Isabel seemed troubled. She'd been having difficulties with Elena, one of her friends from school. Elena's mother was killed when their car careened off the side of the road; Elena was just a baby, strapped in her car seat in the back. Since then, Elena's father, who was driving, had remarried: he had a perky, pediatrician wife and a young son. At school events, he seemed unscathed, as if he had lost nothing. But Elena seemed hammered by the loss.

"Elena says it's better that she can't remember her mother," Isabel told me once. "Do you think it's better?"

"Any way you lose your mother isn't good."

Elena was writing a book about her friends at school, and she would dangle their fates before them, to taunt them. But they liked her. She was funny and smart and tough.

Too tough, in fact. She had crossed a line with Isabel, and things became physical: she would spill a drink on her at lunch, and Isabel would be drenched for the rest of the day. She would borrow money and never pay it back. Suddenly, she would stop speaking to Isabel. And just as suddenly, be verbose, affectionate. At a slumber party, she dumped a drink all over Isabel's sleeping bag, dousing it, and Isabel slept in it, wet.

"Isn't that what female bullying looks like?" I asked my shrink.

"That's not bullying. That's abuse."

"Abuse?"

"Yes, because Isabel is in a relationship with this person. There's intimacy. That's abuse, when you draw someone in, when they trust you, and you betray them."

When you draw someone in, when they trust you, and you betray them.

How come I didn't know that Isabel was being abused? I didn't even know the *meaning* of the word "abuse."

All I knew was that Isabel seemed unhappy, so I jumped in. "Sweetie, what's going on?"

"Nothing."

"You don't seem okay."

"It's nothing."

"Daddy and I are here. We want to help."

Day after day, I would ask Isabel the same question: "What's going on?" Her answer was always the same: "I'm fine" or "I don't want to talk about it" or "I'll take care of it." Michael and I urged her to confront Elena, but she refused, and she begged us not to intervene.

Then I got a call from school. "Your daughter seems anxious. Is something happening at home?"

"No," I said, startled by the call, by the question. But I thought I knew what was going on. "Someone at school is bothering her." I stopped, unsure whether to identify the child. "I've never had a conversation like this before. Do I tell you her name?"

"Of course," the teacher said.

"It's Elena," I told her.

"We'll take care of it."

She stepped in and insisted that Elena stop abusing Isabel. And Elena stopped.

* * *

It was that simple. That's how easily someone could have saved me from Joe. Help could have come swiftly, without recrimination. I never imagined that was possible. People routinely rescue other people, I know now, from my research. Neuroscientists believe that, as a species, we have evolved to communicate feeling and show empathy. Love rewires us from the time we are infants, influencing the expression of genes and altering the very architecture of the brain. (Talk about remodeling!) Love makes us who we are.

A month or so later, Isabel said she and Elena were friends again. "She has her moments, when she loses it," Isabel told me. She thought for a moment and smiled. "But don't we all?"

"That depends."

"Losing it" could mean many things. Would Isabel know if she was in danger?

"What does she do when she 'loses it?'" I asked.

"She cries, and I just sit there and keep her company." She smiled and shrugged. "I think that's what she needs."

We had long thought of Charlotte as our resident empath—as well as our GPS system—but Isabel was lighting a path to forgiveness and generosity.

"This friendship thing is hard to figure out," she said softly.

"I'm *still* trying to figure it out."

"It's different. You have Daddy."

"So?"

"I don't have anyone who feels about me the way he feels about you."

46.

I thought about the alchemy required for two people to understand each other, and the near-impossibility that they ever
really do. Scientists can chart the neural pathways of love: on an
MRI scan, they can see certain portions of the brain light up when
a subject looks at his or her beloved. As Diane Ackerman has written, holding the hand of one's partner can decrease blood pressure
and relieve pain.

Maybe that's what haunted Simon most: that Lacey had sev-
ered their bond so precipitously, irrevocably. That she hadn't trusted
him, or anyone, to help. I could imagine him, years after Lacey's
death, standing in a squash court, lost in thoughts of the awful time
he'd tried to teach her to play. I suspect the violence of that day never
left him. Nor, I imagined, would the violence of her final act.

Maybe, in his reverie, he remembered the first time he saw
her, at the policy meeting in London. She probably seemed much
more vivid, more alive, than anyone else. Maybe, on their first
date, she even spoke of her fears: that she wasn't smart enough,
that she might not finish her degree. She had seemed so open, so
winning. Maybe that's when he fell in love with her.

Yes, she had been distraught. (He learned that later from his research.) The weight loss? Depression. So, too, the sleeplessness. Maybe all she had needed was better medical attention. Maybe all she had needed was more rest. Maybe he wondered, all these years later, why she had done it. But it didn't matter, did it: why it happened. She had made it happen with her force of will. The same will that revealed itself in restaurants when she wanted a better table. It was even a bit embarrassing. That combination of charm and force that had propelled her so far.

She had taken what they had, "the two-edness" of them, and destroyed it in one terrible moment: their shared interests. Their silent jokes. But maybe that bond—so avid, so private—had been broken earlier, much earlier, when she was suffering, and he didn't see it. When she decided not to tell him, to let him in.

"Why did you move back to England?" I asked Simon, in our last conversation.

"My lease was ending." Then, after a moment, "I had met someone . . . I met her through another set of friends a bit more than a year after Lacey died."

For me, this information presented as a small earthquake. I didn't know he had met Sara in California. I didn't know she was American. I wondered at my response: Was it because I felt some loyalty to Lacey that I couldn't believe she was so easily replaced?

"A year and a half after a death, you've asked so many questions. And you've come to no particular conclusion, other than that you'll never know. I joined several suicide groups in California," he said, brightening now. "After a while, you see new people keep coming in. They're really raw. They see no future for themselves. You think, 'I'm not like that anymore.' Things start to look up. You realize, 'I'm not thinking about it every waking moment.'"

He was thinking about Sara.

He continued to brighten. "In a purely selfish way, being part of that group has diminishing returns. 'Why didn't I see the signs? Why didn't I understand depression? Why didn't I buy a book about it?' The need to keep going over those questions diminishes. It's no longer very valuable."

"Do you ever think about Lacey?"

"Not a lot. Sometimes I have dreams about her. She's alive, and I'm kind of annoyed. She ran off. It's highly intrusive. Now that I have a new family, kids, I'm actually more angry than I ever was with her."

His candor and fearlessness were breathtaking. He wasn't censoring himself. He wasn't trying to seem neutral or considerate. He was just—to use the word he kept punching up—"alive." I thought about Kyle, who taught Simon to Rollerblade. They were moving forward—on wheels, no less.

They would not forget Lacey, but they would not allow her loss to fester. This is what it means to let go, to heal.

Simon said "yes" to beginning again—to England, to Sara, to children, to resuming his life sadder, richer, resigned but relieved, too. He had allowed himself to grieve, and now his days were simpler; he was no longer stranded in what he called the "deep waters" of emotional turmoil and family strife. There was a sense that he may never have really known Lacey. Maybe that's why she sometimes intruded upon his sleep. He walked right up to the edge of her anguish, two solitudes bordering each other, but he could not see past the surface brightness to the darkness below. He never knew Lacey, but in some way, she had not allowed him to know her. Did others? Did she really know herself? Maybe even she did not realize the depth of her anguish. That was something we will never really know.

Simon said "yes," but Lacey could not. She had accepted his proposal—the enormity of marriage may have been part of her undoing—but she could not say "yes" to the uncertainty inherent in love. She sensed the heartbreak around the edges, loitering there, like a coyote in the garden, but she could not embrace it or shoo it away. She did not know, perhaps, how strong she was, that she could have survived disappointment; that she could have left

Chatsworth, told her family, found a therapist. And then, maybe, she might have had a child, and a garden. Maybe she might have written another book.

I knew my talk with Simon would be my final call about Lacey. I, too, was ready to move on. It no longer mattered why Risa would not return my phone calls, or whether Anson Bishop misunderstood the nature of my inquiries. Perhaps he worried that I wanted something, or knew something; when he discovered I did not, he felt no need to get back in touch. But perhaps there were moments, when his secretary was placing a call, and his eye fell on a company photo, or when he was traveling and he looked out the window of the airplane, into blue. Perhaps, in those moments, he thought of Lacey, and missed her. That was all I really wanted to know.

There was nothing petulant in this, only accepting. There was nothing to be gained, no more to be known. Why Lacey leapt, why success catches anyone by the throat, makes her feel she cannot breathe, cannot be normal, was both too easy to imagine and forever beyond our ken. The people who survive the jump from the Golden Gate Bridge, almost without exception, realize only when they let go of the railing that all problems can be solved. All but this. Maybe Lacey, too, sensed it could not be undone once done, and so hesitated to do it, extending her stay in the hotel three separate times. Maybe she was reading the Sunday newspaper from cover to cover, to see if anything might compel her to try again.

Part of the pain of her loss is the finality of it; there is no going back, once it has been done. The calculus of grief is transfixing, but also infuriating. There is no knowing why. She herself may not have known. Was she depressed? Anxious? Ailing from her car accident? Was the accident a mistake, a bad dream from which she could not awaken? She had been working all night, at a job she could not master. Was she feeling hopeless, or just fatigued? Lacey had no reason; she had every reason: she was afraid; she had never been happier; Simon was coming; Simon should have come sooner. There was a chair. She was relaxed; she had been reading the Sunday paper, cover to cover. She was wearing a business suit. Someone wanted her briefcase. Her briefcase was bare. Distilled, the elements form a haiku of obfuscation, of frustration. She leaves behind a poem of scrambled facts. And a note, which even Simon acknowledged was "not the best thing she ever wrote." Her suicide note is judged, and found wanting. Now it is lost.

Weeks before, when I first spoke to Lacey's brother, I said I'd read that people saved from suicide invariably regret their decision to die. After ninety days, the crisis has passed, and they trudge on. I can remember saying it, and hearing his silence deepen on the other end of the phone. Who would want to know that their beloved sister might have been saved, if she told someone, if someone had known? It was the only grave error in all my conversations, the only moment I wished I could have taken back. I had said something so casual, not meant to be hurtful, but so wounding I could almost hear the incision ooze.

I wanted to undo it, the minute it was said, as so many people did once they had jumped. They wanted to unleap. How many times had Lacey stood on that chair, on the balcony of the hotel, and looked over at her own apartment, perhaps, or out at the city, willing herself back to the bed to rest, to stay?

If she had lived, she might have looked back at that moment as her greatest triumph, when she faced anguish and desolation and disillusionment.

And stepped away.

Now I would have to step away, too; to let go of Lacey, though I felt closer to her than to the neighbor whose eucalpytus shed in our yard. I would let go of her sister, hoping she would find a measure of peace one day. Hoping that she and her brother would reconcile, with each other and with the past. "Forgiveness liberates the soul. It removes fear. That's why it is such a powerful weapon," Nelson Mandela said. It was this Lacey's husband had taught me above all. Despite his professed ignorance of the "deep waters" of emotional complexity, this social scientist had learned to swim. He knew he needed to forgive, or he would never be free.

47.

I hoped Michael and I could move forward, too. That he could forgive me for being so useless when he was sick. There was still so much warmth between us, and gratitude for our daughters. But I could sense a muscle memory of abandonment. In general, Michael was very good at forgetting things. The first time I took my parents to see his office, my father returned from the men's room: "Someone's suit jacket was hanging in my stall. It was a very nice suit."

Michael was not at all surprised, but he was thankful: "I've been looking for that all day!"

When Isabel was a baby, and friends were driving behind us on the way to the park, Michael left his wallet on top of the car; he was literally *throwing away money;* we watched the dollars dance and circle like contrails in the wake of the car.

So I shouldn't have been surprised when we were invited to a fancy Hollywood party—and showed up on the wrong day. We stood alone on the expansive lawn, gaping at its emptiness. Those valets who present you with a rose when they return your car? They weren't there. Nor were the requisite gleaming flunkeys, who restrain the requisite mastiffs, or the actress/models who pass hors d'oeuvres while passing judgment on *you.* We looked around, stunned and disbelieving, for the starlets fresh from their facial peels, for the cascades of tropical flowers, for the plush outdoor sofas that had suddenly become *de rigueur*.

When we got home, Michael slumped in a chair, slowly untying the bow tie he had carefully constructed, like a work of origami, only hours before.

"I goofed," he said.

"It doesn't matter."

"Do you want to go out to eat or something? We have a babysitter."

"No. You seem tired. Let's just stay home."

"But you're all dressed up."

"So are you." I looked more closely. "Well, I mean, you *were*."

I realized he had taken off his shirt, and I could see where the radiation technician had tattooed him, so his torso could be lined up perfectly, day after day. Sometimes he came home from treatment with skin so scorched it was raw.

"C'mon," I said. "I have an idea."

I led him gently by the hand, down the stairs and into the garden, dense with the smell of eucalyptus. I could hear the staccato of crickets in the canyon below. On Saturday nights there was always music coming from the canyon, but by now our daughters could sleep through anything, their bodies pale against the pale pink sheets.

"Here," I put my arms around Michael, and we began to move slowly, awkwardly. Gradually, we let go, laughing, falling over our feet. "Sadness is a path between two gardens," the Buddhists say, and maybe that's true: a path between the garden at Oxford, where I slowly circumambulated with my mother, and this garden now. Now I knew so much more about reconciliation and forgiveness.

I drew Michael closer, steadying him.

That's what it was about, wasn't it, Rilke's solitudes, bordering, greeting each other. Never merging. That's what most of us mistake about love. You can't melt into anyone else, any more than you can like jalapeños, just because he does. (Yes, spicy foods correlate to longer life, but you will shore yourself up in other ways.) In the years since his treatment, Michael had suffered two bouts of pneumonia—the radiation temporarily weakened his immune system—but he was well now. We could make things right between us. I wanted to make them right. I hoped we would have a long, long time together, the time Lacey and Simon never had.

I thought back to our first real dance, at our wedding, when we forgot all the steps we had practiced over many months, coached by a man with glittering nails and a toupee. Now, I was much more at home in Michael's arms.

Now, his arms were home.

I could feel how this moment connected us to something deeper, to a sense of touch that seemed almost primal. For touch was our first language, before words. It is touch, the laying on of hands, that links us—there is no separation—weaving together our fate and the fate of others, everywhere we turn.

"Language is only a little thing sitting on top of this huge ocean of movement," Oliver Sacks once said. For so long, words were my weapons, defending me against touch. For so long, touch was crushing, eviscerating. But now Michael was here: his arms, my necklace, at last. This was the *pas de deux* I'd longed for, his bare chest brushing the silk of my gown. This was the real dance, the dance of belonging.

I knew its choreography by heart.

I became who I am because of loving Michael. Because of being loved by him. "Your heart has to keep breaking until it opens," the poet Rumi wrote. Psychobiologists say you have to choose agency, engagement: disabling the brain's "rage pathway" by engaging the "seeking" one. (Both cannot fire at once.) All I knew was that I was finally ready not to be gripped by fear any longer. Not to be gripped by anything, but to be *held* by love. To be dancing: twirling, laughing, the owls hooting their approval, as our daughters watched from the window, their faces flourescent as the moon.

48.

That is what shapes us, *saves* us, that dance of belonging: as complex as a quadrille, as steady as a march. In teenage girls, engagement measurably increases self-esteem. For sufferers of depression, opening out to others soothes and animates the self.

I might have learned this lesson years ago, at the Rhodes reunion, in Aristotle's belief that happiness involves deploying one's gifts for the larger good. Or further back, when the abuse counselor told me: "Use what happened to you to help someone else." She thought my experience could give me range and feeling for what others had suffered, suffering far greater than mine.

So, on my birthday, I volunteered at a charter elementary school on skid row. I sat on the floor and talked with kids about writing stories, and helped them write stories of their own.

When it was time to leave, Mona, the teacher who had brought me there, told me about a little girl who hadn't been in one of my classes. Her mother was twenty-seven years old and already had five children; the oldest was twelve.

"Last week we had to call social services," Mona told me. "The little girl came to school with welts on her back."

"What's her name?"

"Angelia," she said, giving the name its lilting Spanish pronunciation. "Maybe you can meet her next time."

"I want to meet her now."

Then, standing before me, was tiny Angelia, much smaller than the boisterous, affectionate fourth and fifth graders I had been working with. She looked terrified, and I remembered seeing her outside the classroom earlier, wary of entering. I launched in.

"Mona tells me you're a writer, a wonderful writer, and I'd love to see what you're writing. I saw you earlier, outside the door, and I could tell that you were very special. Would you like to get together, to talk about writing? We could have lunch or something. Or tea."

Angelia did not look up. Maybe she doesn't have access to a computer, for writing or making plans. I chastised myself for forgetting what the limitations of her life might be. But I wanted to reach out to her.

"Should I write down my phone number or my email address?"

She looked up for the first time. "Both."

Something about her glistening eyes compelled me. I leaned down close to her. "Angelia, I want to say something to you. I grew up in a difficult family; it was like I landed from another planet, from outer space."

Mona laughed uncomfortably.

"They didn't understand me. They didn't understand my writing or anything. They didn't take care of me. They didn't protect me."

The words were coming faster now, more freely, even as Angelia's eyes turn downward again. I couldn't believe I was saying all this, and to a child.

I had never said these words aloud before.

"But here I am. I'm okay. And it was the writing that helped me. It was the writing that got me here. You'll be okay, too."

I could feel her receding.

"May I put my arms around you?" I asked, loathe as I am, ever, to touch anyone, to be touched.

She leaned in, almost against her will.

"Does it feel okay to be hugged?"

She did not respond, but she did not move away.

"Let's meet and talk about writing, okay? Or anything you want to talk about."

"Can I come?" Mona asked merrily.

Then Angelia was gone.

Weeks later, when her father beat her again, Angelia came to school and told Mona, and Mona told Maria, the school principal, who had grown up in this neighborhood, shielded from gunfire by an older brother. Maria called the police. The INS came to the tiny apartment—seven people sleeping in a single room—and arrested Angelia's father. They threatened to deport him, and for days no one knew if they would see him again. Her siblings—two brothers and two sisters—were furious at Angelia for betraying the family. At night, the sister with whom she shared a bed pummeled her with her fists. But the father returned, and I saw him months later, at Angelia's fifth grade graduation. He was compact and grinning, surprisingly gregarious.

"Your daughter is very special," I told him, and he smiled broadly.

I wondered if he knew I *knew*.

"I want to do something for Angelia," I told Mona as the graduation was ending. "Like foster her or something."

"She needs to stay with her family," Mona insisted, as if she'd considered the possibility herself.

As I drove home, past the blighted buildings, I realized Mona was right. Angelia needed to stay in the world she knew. All I could do was encourage her, listen to her talk about her dreams and her friends and her favorite foods. All she wanted was for someone to see her. That's all I'd ever wanted, too. "Live in fragments no longer," E. M. Forster wrote, in a line much less celebrated than his admonition to connect. That's what I had been seeking; what Angelia was seeking, too. Not an escape, not an excuse, not an evidentiary hearing. Something more basic, galvanic: the chance to be whole.

I thought about the girl at my high school who'd approached me gingerly when I screened my movie. Someone was hurting her, and she couldn't tell anyone, even though *I* could tell.

I had done nothing to help her. But maybe I could help Angelia.

In the months that followed, Angelia's father left the family for good, and Angelia began writing dozens of poems. I took her to lunch and to the craft store; sent her journals; wore a tiny bracelet of plastic hearts she made for me.

I learned later that she, too, had been suicidal.

Another girl looking for a way out.

But Angelia made a different choice: to tell someone; to save her family, even if they didn't know it yet, even if her brothers and sisters blamed her for sending their *papi* away. She had protected them without sacrificing herself; if anything, she was stronger. She would go on writing, drawing, designing dresses late at night, in bed. For many months, she sent me letters:

Dear Jessica

I read your letter thanks for the doggy [eraser]. I really love you as my best friend because you and Ms. Mona have done something really special in my life. Today at the fieldtrip was so alsome. Today I saw that your friend, you, Ms. Mona and me were waering white shirt. I realy wanted to thank you for everything you are doing for me!! Ok do you know what I really really want to do is shop for clothes or school meterials. I LOVE YOU!! You are like my mother!!

Your daughter (just kidding),
Angelia

Over time, Angelia and I fell out of touch. Then I received another email from her:

> *I miss you! I'm good. Thank God, I've been able to overcome obstacles. And I'm proud of myself for becoming a young woman who has learned to mature and be strong in rough times. My family is good . . . me and my mom have a much better relationship and communication. How are you? I wanted to get a hold of you. And I finally found this email, which I doubted at first that it would work! But I'm really happy that I'm able to talk to you again even though it's through an email. I've just been wanting to thank you Jessica. You helped me become the girl I am now. Not only did you believe in me but you loved me when I needed love. Thank you.*

After the long silence, I was thrilled to hear from her, to know she was well, and to learn that I had helped her. "Whoever saves a life, it's as if one saves the entire world," it says in the Talmud. No greater honor could be conferred. But it was Angelia who had saved her own life, by reaching out, by trusting. By doing what Lacey never could: asking for help.

PART SIX

THE CONSOLATIONS OF BELONGING

This thing of darkness I
Acknowledge mine.
                    —William Shakespeare

49.

Angelia, aptly named for an angel, had pointed to a kind of clarity, a way out that was also a way in. But it was Lacey's impact that made the world seem brighter, more benevolent. There was more space, suddenly, between me and the sky.

That meant I was ready to face perhaps the most vexing test of my sanity: remodeling. There was a lot of "deferred maintenance" in our canyon house. (How these house metaphors resonate!) We needed to shore up our home's foundation. To paint over some bad patches. To provide more insulation from what in California passes for cold.

Remodeling meant cleaning out the house, the garage, my office; packing up my files on Lacey: Rhodes paraphernalia and articles on why Americans and Germans are more prone to crying than Bulgarians or the Chinese. Most precious were the transcripts of calls with those who loved her, which I had transcribed long-hand on legal pads. (Ever the Luddite, I could never get the tape recorder to work.)

From time to time I would re-read the interviews, remembering the freshness of Kyle's voice, his little boy earnestness; Corinne's caginess; Simon's frustration with Lacey, his grief. Each, of course, had his or her own agenda: Kyle, to protect his sister; Corinne, to protect herself; Simon, to protect his new family, or so it seemed.

Over time, the file boxes, borrowed from Michael's law firm, had proliferated like a mutant plant form. They towered over me, menacing obelisks blocking out the sun.

I never expected this woman to besiege my life. Where had all the time gone? It was as if I had been bewitched.

For too many months, the Lacey odyssey had consumed me. Or perhaps more truly: It had given me yet another reason to say "no." Not to go to the park or to the movies with my children; not to curl up next to Michael and watch TV. Meanwhile, life was *happening*; multiple forms of technology becoming obsolete even before I could pretend to master them. But most important, my children were growing—changes I could see in them, but never in myself—even as the *files* kept growing, piled so high I could not see the view.

Then one day I walked up the narrow steps to my office, and blinked. Light flooded the tiny room. All the file boxes were gone.

In the endless construction on our house, had someone thrown them out? If they had, would I feel devastation or relief?

Someone had moved the files, thinking they were Michael's, dropping them haphazardly at the foot of a temporary wall. They listed there, looking forlorn.

I threw off the top of one box, then another, searching frantically for my notes.

What I found instead were the essays Michael had written for Bert Dreyfus's philosophy class at Berkeley. Stones he collected on the beach of Lady Elliot Island, where he'd camped for several magical days. And here, printed on perforated computer paper— *that's* how long ago it was—were answers to questions our rabbi asked on the eve of our marriage.

Michael had wrapped them in the tablecloth from our very first date, on which I had drawn the Corvette and the cat and the sixty-three steps. I couldn't believe he had saved it, faded though it was: soft and fraying and spotted with wine.

But what moved me most were his responses to the dyspeptic rabbi's questions, which I had never read before.

I have reprinted them here with his blessing, for they are blessings indeed.

What do you hope to derive from your marriage?
A shared life. Both in the day-to-day comfort and deep pleasure that come from being in the world with someone, and in the shared inner life and intimacy.

Family. A feeling of family (which is really what I described above) and the more literal notion of family— becoming parents.

Why are you marrying this person?
I do not believe there are "reasons" for marrying. Certainly not ones that can be reduced to a list or an essay. Having said that, let me answer the question. (This is all very Michael-like in its lawyerly specificity.)

Because I love Jessica. Early in our relationship I had what I took to be an insight. The feelings I had for Jessica led me to it. I wrote it down one morning sitting in my office . . . It suddenly occurred to me that I finally understood why people marry: it is because the feeling of love is so unbordered and yet so dense that it is impossible to express it by any other act. Any words, any gifts, any other acts would be inadequate approximations of the feeling. I realized my feelings for Jessica could only find their expression through being lived out over a lifetime. Each of our moments together, from the mundane to the life-defining, would be the articulation of my love for her. Each would have as its source, as its meaning, my feeling for Jessica. Each child, each fight, each good night kiss. Trips to the dry cleaners. Growing old, dying.

Nor do I believe that the feelings are used up or depleted through giving life to each of these moments. My love for Jessica has only grown larger as we have grown closer.

What woman wouldn't swoon at such a man, and such a marriage? Why had I been so terrified?

50.

⁓

Weeks later, I received an invitation to speak at an event celebrating the thirtieth anniversary of the first female Rhodes scholars. Women would converge on Oxford from around the globe and across decades to commemorate the biggest single change in the history of the Trust. The weekend would feature dinner parties and panel discussions, a keynote address in the Sheldonian Theatre, and a chance to sleep in your old bed. This last was hardly tempting, since I didn't want to sleep in that bed even when it was the only bed I had. But I appreciated the sentiment.

Most of all, I appreciated the chance to share my thoughts about "life in the creative arts," about women and power and progress.

Still, it seemed ironic to take a public forum to extol the virtues of private life, of happiness cobbled together beyond professional success, mixed with loss. To say how grateful I was, not to have succumbed like Lacey, but to have found peace and Prozac and the pleasures of owning a dog. Happiness is real, but what lasts is some sense of rootedness, of lining up one's self-image with the patterns of daily life. We are all startled by a view of ourselves from another angle, as in a department store mirror that captures us from another side, a side we did not see. How do we create a persona that is flexible, easy, accommodating, that allows us to be all the things we are?

We took the trip as a family, a kind of bonding mission, to strengthen our ties after the challenges of the past few months. Our daughters had never been overseas, and I wondered if they would miss California. If they would miss the sun.

But it was Michael who never warmed to England, declaring, even as he emerged from the plane, "No wonder the British don't have a space program; the way the toilet is designed, it can't even flush!"

He remained skeptical throughout our stay: "The English have seen the integrated faucet and they're sticking with the separate hot and cold. Even *I* don't want to fill a public basin to wash my hands." Isabel picked up on his attitude, but sweetly, reading aloud from a guidebook: "In the British Library Reading Room you can see the eleventh century will of Athelstan the Atheling son of Ethelred the Unready, who left his worldly goods to, among others, Aethelweard the Stammerer and Godwine the Driveller." Gleefully, she collected the names of unappetizing-sounding restaurants: The Slug and Lettuce, The Squat and Gobble.

But Charlotte found the whole experience unsettling, nonplussed by a language she thought she understood. She would mull over the strange words—"loo" and "lorry" and "jumper"—and insisted on calling the department store Harrods "Harriets." Isabel tried to help, reading to her from the guidebook, pointing out that the lions in Trafalgar Square were modeled on the artist's Labradors. No one in London had *seen* an actual lion back then, but that only made Charlotte more homesick; she was missing Emma the dog so much.

From London it was on to Oxford. We arrived at dusk, strolling the winding streets, the students surging past in their subfusc. Isabel turned back to have a bath, while Michael and I headed to

Magdalen to see the Deer Park at twilight, Charlotte racing ahead in her "trainers" (purchased at "Harriets"). The three of us stood silently, watching the deer graze, beguiled by their beauty. Charlotte seemed to breathe deeply for the first time in days. I didn't have the heart to tell her *why* there was a Deer Park: to provide fresh meat for visiting royalty.

Beyond the park, past the "new" buildings (built in the early 1730s), lay the river, where a lonely punt waited for a reprieve. As we walked back toward the college, Charlotte shivered. "What are we doing here, Mommy?"

"I used to live here. Before you were born."

"Were you here when they built these buildings?"

"No. They're even older than I am."

"They *are?*"

"Yes, they were built before the Revolution. Remember Felicity, the American Girl doll?"

But a German tourist interrupted to ask a mystifying question: "*Entschuldigung,* do you know how much the Magdalen Tower weighs?"

As we walked toward that tower, Charlotte whispered under her breath, "It's creepy." Oxford's spires, so legendarily dreamy, were for her too thorny, too crepuscular. I tried to see this world through her eyes, all the gothic spikes and seething gargoyles. It must have seemed positively penitentiary-like. (She hadn't discovered *Harry Potter,* yet.) But for me, Oxford had been C. S. Lewis's place of "visions and loosening chains." Even in the bleakest moments, the Cotswold stone held a buttery glow. Years ago, I had chosen Magdalen not just for its stellar academic record, but because it was pronounced "Maudlin," a description that I thought also suited me. Happily, I had changed, but the college hadn't. I'd forgotten how beautiful it was.

"Are you sure we're supposed to be here?"

"Charlotte . . . " Michael growled, with the unspecific menace parents master early on.

But I could tell that she was genuinely afraid. So I marched

into the Porter's Lodge, a dank little loggia with a warren of cub-
bies for mail and the local messages known as "pigeon post." The
porter, with gaping holes where his teeth should be, welcomed us.

"We've come all the way from Florida!" I exclaimed. I meant
to say "California." *That's* how tired I was.

"I didn't know you were from Florida!" Charlotte marveled.

Michael leaned in gently. "Sweetie, you're not in the witness
protection program anymore."

"Is there any mail for me?" I asked hopefully, and Michael
laughed. The porter immediately went to the computer to look me up.

"Teich," he said thoughtfully. "You came to us from Yale.
Read English."

Charlotte looked impressed.

"In residence from 1981 to 1983."

"Yes."

"Any mail we had would have been forwarded on."

Michael was pleased by how seriously he took my inquiry.
I hoped Charlotte would be, too. I wanted her to feel that we
belonged here. *I* belonged here, still. But it is not one's name in
a computer that creates a sense of legitimacy. How do we find
a home in the world? For me, a feeling of belonging had always
proved elusive, and I worried that my daughters had sensed my
displacement, even inherited it.

In that moment, I realized why I'd brought my family here,
for it was here that I first felt a sense of family. I wanted them to
know that this, too, was part of my past, this glorious place, where
I first discovered the balm of genuine friendship, the goofy rapture
of late-night tennis on the sodden lawn. Oxford was the beginning
of my grown-up life. Here, I could step into my own skin. And
here, for the first time, I found others who were like me: loners,
misfits, longing to connect.

What I will always remember, more than meeting the Queen
in my long red gloves (I had just finished writing about Lady
Macbeth's bloody digits) was the sharing of benign secrets over

Indian curry from the Cowley Road. Long walks in the Botanic Gardens and raucous games of Scrabble and the toothy reassurance of Mary Tyler Moore. These were the unsuspected consolations of belonging: cheerful glints of conviviality, of grace. Though my children were born in a land without seasons, they are, in part, the daughters of that winter. For it was then that my isolation began to melt.

51.

✑

"Everyone's soul has a place where it feels at home," said a quiet voice next to me. I was at the formal dinner in Rhodes House, presided over by a portrait of Cecil Rhodes. Rhodes himself was legendarily wimpy; he insisted on lifelong vigor for his scholars but died in his forties. Yet here he was, looking like a buccaneer, or a Tommy Hilfiger model, in his pressed linen breeches and leather boots.

Nearby and newly installed was a painting of Nelson Mandela—resplendent in kente cloth—for whom the building we were sitting in had just been renamed. On the Rhodes's centenary, a fund was established to bring more Africans to Oxford, as a significant gesture of investment in South Africa—the original source of the Trust's endowment—and to honor the principal architect of that country's transformation, Mandela, its first black president. The Rhodes will always be a fortune built on enormous crime: "in slavery, like America," as one woman put it, provocatively. But one hundred years on, it was no longer just an instrument "to inculcate the retrograde values of the motherland." In fact, as one young woman observed: "There were more gay men in our class than Republicans. Now you can be married; in fact, the only person in my class who was married was a man married to another man."

"The legacy of Rhodes women has been established in three short decades," the warden of Rhodes House intoned at the start of the celebration. "It's an impressive evolution; a transformation, you might say. Cecil Rhodes gave the money. He gave us a little bit of his DNA, too."

But the DNA of the audience was decidedly female. If there were husbands and sons here—let alone male Rhodes scholars—they were not visible. My own family had decamped to punt on the Cherwell, an adventure that would remain alive for many years after, given that Michael had to do battle with a cantankerous duck.

At the dinner, I was seated next to a lithe young woman, elegant and soft-spoken, with a stray tooth that marred her perfect countenance. "Kathleen," she said when asked her name, in the soft staccato of South Africa. She grew up on the karoo, a massive part of the country's heartland, with three brothers and sisters, and a young mother who homeschooled them, letting them run wild in the outback, without shoes. "Everyone's soul has a place where it feels at home," she said again, almost dreamily.

"Is England that place for you?" I asked.

"No," she laughed softly. "It is my natural condition to have space. I feel as if someone's taken it away."

"Do you ever think of going back?"

"I live with a man, another South African. He's also a Rhodes scholar. He doesn't wish to go back."

"Why not?"

"It's difficult for an Afrikaans man, because of the situation. The violence. He's afraid, I guess."

"Are you?"

"Where I grew up, in Grahamstown, there was no violence." She was silent for a moment. "And I'm not afraid."

I thought of Lacey when I looked around the table at the faces of the young women, illuminated by candles, laughing loudly, cheeky and unbowed.

"I still remember the absurd boasts of men in various Rhodes settings," one woman was saying. "They were always insisting, 'I'm working on democratization in such-and-such,' and I would find myself asking, 'What countries have democratized as a result of your attention to the subject?!'"

Their flippancy about the Rhodes was unusual but also welcome—heretical and delightful both.

Yet Kathleen seemed tentative, even reluctant; her boldness stippled with something like regret.

What frightened her, it turned out, was her uncertainty about this man. Was he meant to be her husband? The father of her kids? Kathleen revealed that her mother died several months ago, and her large, luminous eyes filled with tears.

"How terrible to go out of the world with young children left behind," I said softly.

She nodded. "But she knew we would be okay."

The dinner was interrupted periodically by bursts of speech, by jokes and toasts, by formal salutes to the founder and the Queen. Each time our conversation resumed, it took us deeper into her uncertainty. She seemed eloquent, poised, even peaceful, but lost.

"There's another man," she began. "I find myself dreaming about him. We're just friends. But I have so many things I want to talk to him about. He was involved with someone else, but they broke up. I'm not sure what he's feeling these days. I want to see him. I want to *tell* him I want to see him."

"Why don't you?"

"I could never do that to my boyfriend."

"Do you love your boyfriend?" I couldn't believe I was asking her that.

"I don't feel whatever I'm supposed to feel. But he's smart. And kind. My father likes him very much. And we have so much in common, being Rhodes scholars and all.

"I just can't wait to talk to him, whenever I see him." She was talking about the other man. "I think he feels that way, too."

"That's what you want to find," I urged her. "Someone to talk to. I think that's all there is."

"But how do you know?" she wondered, and I heard longing in her voice, for her mother, for the karoo.

Lacey found a man at Oxford who loved her, who was funny and stable and attentive, if limited. He knew very little about the "deep waters" of emotional complexity. Lacey, he thought, could teach him about that. But learning to navigate those waters could take a lifetime, unless you are a natural, like Charlotte, floating down. For Isabel, finding a home may be harder, and I wanted her to give herself time. And freedom, the freedom Lacey never had.

"Don't rush," I reassured Kathleen. "Don't be hurried. Tell this friend, this other man, how you feel."

"Oh, I couldn't."

"Well, *see* him. See what it's like with him."

Otherwise, your soul will never be safe.

Just then, the warden urged us to disband, given the early start of tomorrow's panels. Kathleen and I rose slowly from the table, awkward, unwilling to leave.

Before we parted, Kathleen told me she had just bought herself a copy of Rilke's *Letters to a Young Poet,* in which he advised that one must live the questions until the day the answers announce themselves. That was precisely what I would have wanted to tell her.

Do not be afraid.

Something about my encounter with Kathleen haunted me, long after we left the table, even though we never spoke again. I was moved by her desire to be true to something, vast and unknowable as the karoo, that she had a sense of but could not name.

Kathleen wanted to live the questions, unafraid of their ambiguity. There was something victorious, *numinous,* in that. She was the person Lacey might have been; Isabel might become; another young woman, reaching toward a shimmer on the horizon.

Do not be afraid.

52.

⟡

The next morning, my fellow panelist was Diahnna, a gorgeous, dark-skinned woman in her thirties, who beamed when asked how she wanted to be introduced. "Renaissance gal," she said boldly. "Or creative dynamo. Either one is fine."

"And you?" The moderator turned to me.

"Mother. And writer," I said. I handed her one of the mock business cards I had printed recently, which listed my bona fides: Mother. Writer. *Driver.* "Roads scholar" indeed.

Diahnna smiled at me, and I remembered reading her lengthy résumé: medical doctor and entrepreneur and jazz musician and painter and the minister of culture in her native Bahamas. She'd brought copies of her CDs and slides of her paintings, spreading them out on the table before us. (I kept a copy of my little book tucked in my purse.)

"I've crossed three, four, five, six career divides," Diahnna said to kick off the panel. "I've learned that self-justification is completely unnecessary. Your only job is to be yourself. The biographical bits, they have nothing to do with me. I've had to let it go, to move across many levels of consciousness, to find a different paradigm."

Diahnna talked about her experiences as a medical student: seeing patients on the ward, wondering what they were thinking.

"I was one of those patients," I began, when my turn came. "I got sick my first term at Oxford, and ended up at the Neurological Hospital in Queen Square. I lost sensation in my right hand and arm and leg, and I had trouble speaking. That was the moment my life changed. My *feelings* about my life changed."

I told them I thought it was okay to want an "ordinary" life, of lesser scale than the Rhodes all but guaranteed. "Maybe that means we don't have to do so much to impress, to transfigure. We don't have to *do* at all. We can just *be*. Winston Churchill called success 'the ability to go from one failure to another with no loss of enthusiasm.'"

The audience laughed.

"Maybe 'success' is an abstract, even infantile pursuit."

Maybe being a Rhodes scholar isn't the first achievement of adulthood, but the last great gasp of adolescence.

After that, real life seeps in, with all its loss and learning.

Then we discover who we really are.

Earlier that morning, I had entered this room, as someone had advised twenty-five years ago, when I was applying for a Rhodes, to feel the space, and imagine myself in it. I sat down in one of the chairs, surveyed the mahogany-panelled walls, noted the dirty windows, then swivelled to look behind me. On the bookshelves were *hundreds* of Rhodes theses, on subjects ranging from the "rape" of Cinderella to sleep apnea.

I wondered if Lacey's thesis might be there; the one that became her book. Finishing her thesis was the beginning of the end for her, needing to confront real life, beyond the storied cloisters of St. Antony's. Emerson said, "Sometimes a scream is better than a thesis." *Any* thesis.

I wished Lacey had known how to scream.

"One of yesterday's panelists talked about the difference between the 'real' self and the 'public' self," I continued. "But I don't think we need to choose between what's authentic and what isn't. Whatever we choose to do, to *be,* is real. Don't we want that for our daughters, that freedom? How can we heal the world if we can't heal these divisions in ourselves?"

These dichotomies are dangerous, that's what I wanted to tell them. They created the gaps that claimed Lacey, swallowed her whole.

We—not just Rhodes scholars, but *all* women—have held ourselves to a very high standard, but life levels the playing field. According to a report in *The New York Times,* we have fewer hours to ourselves than women in the 1960s, '70s, '80s, and '90s. In fact, working mothers devote about 50 percent more time to child care than nonworking fathers. It turns out that, even in the developed world, the traditional division of labor is still deeply ingrained. "If being a Rhodes scholar gives us anything, it is the confidence to reject notions of performance and accomplishment that fit us as poorly as Cinderella's rags. We can let our lives be fluid, makeshift—as they are bound to be, whether we will it or not. If we can learn to fit the pieces together differently every day, and some days not at all—and also give our partners that freedom—we really will have accomplished something. We will have changed the rules. We will have said that it's okay, not only to want everything, but to want *less* than everything, to want what is intimate in scale, and malleable, and incomplete." I tell them that my understanding of "the world's fight" is different now, twenty-five years after I was chosen. It seems less monolithic, more pliable and open-meshed. "I've come to appreciate the award as a lifelong benefaction. Wherever we are, we can do good."

Even Diahnna weighed in: "The idea of a career, of a consistent narrative, is a fairly recent construct. We've got to let go of trying to weave a continuous thread." I was surprised to hear that from someone so driven. As we got up to go, she kissed me on both cheeks and promised to stay in touch.

I remembered the most rending observation in Lacey's obituary: "Lacey certainly masked a great deal of fear with her gregarious charm. She was not as happy as she seemed in public places." That was perhaps the biggest disconnection, greater even than her inability to see the link between her childhood and her sense of calamity, the familiarity of feeling doomed. "Turn around and look at me," she called to the person who became her closest friend at Oxford, on the night they met.

"Look *into* me," is what she never said.

How lucky we are, any of us, to have had the success we did, to carry it with us, to do it proud, even ever so occasionally. But we are luckier still to have the ordinary life, where we are not asked to perform, to posture; the life where, perhaps, we are just asked to be. Here people love us for the things we did not know to strive for: the smell of our hair, the way we gesture with our hands. And here we have children, who dart like fish into our future.

These were the things Lacey would never have.

"May I hug you?" one young woman asked as the group dispersed. An older woman leaned in, "I think you had Lyme disease. All those years ago. From the Deer Park at Magdalen." She smiled at me conspiratorially.

One young scholar asked me if I thought she should go to India for the summer, or stay in college and write. Would I be willing to read her poems? Another, about to have a baby, wanted me to send her a copy of my book about raising kids. She seemed rattled, overwhelmed. I wanted to reassure them: make mistakes, be subversive, trust yourself, have a little faith. I wrote down their email addresses, and gave them mine, and hugged them, and promised to be in touch.

I thought back to the rousing closing words of the head of Rhodes House: "The legacy of Rhodes women has been established in three short decades. From the first, there were wonderful women, as there are now. There are a thousand different ways to 'fight the world's fight.' We know that now. That fight is still yours to wage."

But it's not always about fight; it's often about endurance. "I guess the lesson is you don't have to be happy all the time," one of the young women allowed. "It's not a sprint, it's a marathon," said another (and she looked like a sprinter). "We each possess the materials to be happy, to make our own space."

I remembered something Kathleen said at dinner the night before: "The buildings are so old. So many people have looked at them. They will never change."

What changes is our ability to see our lives, ourselves, as changing, and to see the fluidity as a boon. Fluidity and longevity, if we are lucky. The freedom to stumble, to screw up. This is everything I have wanted for my daughters: the courage to take chances, to heed their own instincts, to acknowledge their mistakes, to ask for help. Above all, I want to reassure them:

Do not be afraid.

53.

Later that day, my family went to high tea in the unfortunately-named town of Lower Slaughter, in a spot where a house had stood for over a thousand years. The trees were stalwart, sheltering, and Michael was armed with the Wittgenstein biography he was perpetually reading, so he took refuge beneath their boughs.

The girls and I wandered next door to a lopsided little church, stoic in its misshapenness, seeming at once steadfast and haunted by ghosts. It was the parish of a local family; the walls flocked with the names of their dead: "Sebastian" and "Lionel" recurring, on tombstone after tombstone, making up the pattern of the floor. All these people, long dead, yet at peace, or at least, not suffering; their very bodies part of the structure now.

I had wanted to lay a wreath somewhere for Lacey; maybe on the High Street, where she and Simon had married, where she had been happy. But I did not. Instead, I could let her go here, in this little country church, in the presence of my daughters.

Maybe here, she could find some peace.

I had learned so much from Lacey about being porous, allowing the forces of the universe to penetrate. Otherwise we are alone, poised on a chair, looking out over the city.

It is density, intimacy, that keeps us safe.

I thought of a favorite poem, Philip Larkin's "An Arundel Tomb," in which the writer discovers that two of the ancient carved figures are holding hands. The last line is uncharacteristically tender for a man so mordant:

What will survive of us is love.

I was never very good at word games, at puns or anagrams or acrostics, but a simple inversion occurred to me. It could have been the inscription on Lacey's tombstone:

It is love that helps us to survive.

Suddenly there was laughter from the field beyond the church. I ventured out, into the sun.

Isabel was dancing in the long grass, with such energy that Charlotte was transfixed. I stood, watching them, two stars in the same constellation: one in orbit, the other in repose.

"Isabel!" Charlotte screamed.

"Oh my God! What is it?" I cried out.

The place Charlotte pointed to was just a pleasant blur.

But when I thrust my glasses onto my nose, I could see Isabel in the distance, clambering up a fence. Why was she climbing so high, on something so rickety? I couldn't remember when she last had a tetanus shot.

Before I knew it, I was running toward her.

"Isabel, come down! It's not safe!" I wanted to shout. But I did not. She was too far away, and I knew she needed that distance.

She had finally gotten her dénouement.

I watched as she climbed all the way to the top, the rail split by the seasons. She balanced there, one foot in this world, the other in the world beyond.

"Isabel!" Charlotte shouted, and Isabel turned to smile at her.

"Charlotte!" She spread her arms wide, as if her freedom had buoyancy and weight.

Suddenly, there was another shriek.

Something moved, flashing.

A hawk was calling.

Isabel pointed, and Charlotte and I looked up.

We watched the hawk gliding, and Isabel laughed, lost in the sun and the joy of climbing and the pleasure of the moment, as the hawk swooped, glorying in all it could see.

All those months ago, Isabel had been making a dance about brokenness. She had intuited that I—that we—needed to be healed.

Take these sunken eyes and learn to see.

Now here she was, unafraid of the fence, of the hawk, of the moment.

Laying claim to her life, untainted by my fears.

54.

On our way home to L.A., we stayed in New York, the city where I trembled as a child, fearful that Joe might be loitering nearby. In the moonlight, I could see Michael's hands, elegant, with their long, tapered fingers. He was wearing his wedding ring, the one inscribed with the quote from Rilke we loved.

"It's very romantic in New York," I whispered, finding Michael's nipple in the dark.

I felt such tenderness for him, his fitful sleep.

I kissed him—on the face, on the neck, on the mouth—and he responded.

I reached down into his pajamas—their harlequin stripe a source of amusement to our daughters—to feel how hard he was.

Now he was really kissing me.

I remembered reading that, for many parents, sleep was the new sex, but I never knew what that meant, I was so tired. Maybe *sex* could be the new sex for us.

Now Michael was on top of me, kissing me, murmuring, "I really do love you." I feel he really does. I once told Isabel, when she asked about sex, that it was a language two people created together. Michael and I had yet to write our story in bed, and that was exhilarating. So was the warmth of his touch, the sureness of it, the ecstatic feeling of becoming one with him, of belonging to him unhesitatingly. I can't believe I was so resistant to his touch.

After we made love, Michael held my face in his warm hands. I thought of another passage from Rilke that had long been a favorite of his:

> Once the realization is accepted that even between the closest human beings infinite distances continue to exist, a wonderful living side by side can grow up, if they succeed in loving the distance between them which makes it possible for each to see the other whole against the sky.

He'd always said he hoped his illness would bring us closer. Now we were "loving the distance between us," even when my car was parked too close to his in the garage. Everything I valued, Michael had given me: love and acceptance and the freedom to wrinkle the pages of *The New York Times*. He was no consolation prize, this man, this maker of pancakes, this reader of Wittgenstein, who was himself a legendary depressive, although he told his landlady, on his deathbed, "Tell them it's been wonderful." With Michael it *was* wonderful; it always had been; it just took me a long moment to see it. Now I was looking with my heart.

Suddenly there was a figure in the doorway, but I could not make out its features, the darkness different from the darkness in our bedroom at home.

"Who is it?" I whispered.

Silence.

"Isabel?" Michael asked.

"Can I come in?"

"Of course," I said.

We moved aside to make room for her in the hotel bed, in the center between us. Could she felt the heat there? This was the heat that once made her. She snuggled between us; it was so unusual for her to want us, to want to be close to us, to say she needed us, to be willing to ask for help.

"What's going on?" Michael asked.

"I don't know." She burrowed beneath the sheets. "I feel lonely. I guess I miss my friends."

This was triumph: that she could find connection to us, to her friends, to what she was feeling.

In the darkness, I could feel Michael grinning at me.

55.

Once home, we accepted a dinner invitation from our closest friends. I adored them, but I had never eaten at their house. Over the years, Tancredi, a native Roman, had prepared dozens of elaborate dinners: boar ragu—Charlotte promptly became a vegetarian—and many other dishes, on many other Sunday nights. But I always invented a reason to beg off.

I never ate at *anyone's* house, if I could help it. Not a crust of bread. Not an olive (although I hated olives). Not a nut. But now, with Lacey's help, I felt calmer, more controlled, less forgetful, less fretful. It was as if someone had turned on all the lights.

Still, I couldn't convince Isabel to join us.

"Please," she protested, "I just want to stay home."

"What will you do?"

"Read."

"Won't you be lonely? I worry that you spend too much time alone."

"Is there ever enough time alone?" she asked, but she was smiling.

Michael started to protest, but I told him it was okay. She could call us if she needed us. Isabel was old enough to relish her freedom.

Let them be who they are.

When we arrived, Tancredi was chopping tomatoes in the kitchen, wearing a charming if slightly soiled apron. Ruth was setting the table, with sparkling red glasses from the actual set of a Fellini film. Chiara, their daughter and Charlotte's dear friend, was lying on her bed, wary of being asked to serve the Pellegrino and the Parmesan. But more, she was wary of being chided by her mother, as she often was.

"I wish she were a reader," Ruth began, when we were seated. "Two of her friends are readers. Why aren't you reading?"

Chiara looked pained.

"Anyone who thinks they only have one life to live has never read a book," Ruth went on.

"Where did you hear that?" Tancredi asked.

"I *read* it. In the pages of a book!"

Now Ruth turned her attention to Charlotte. "Charlotte, what do *you* care about?"

Charlotte didn't answer immediately, so Ruth said it again, adjusting the emphasis but not the intensity. "Charlotte, what *do* you care about?"

Charlotte looked nonplussed. "Um, my butterflies."

"Butterflies?"

"They're gone, but I loved them. I raised them. They were chrysalisises." She stumbled over the word. "Chrysalises. They were sent to me in the mail."

"The *mail*?"

"For my birthday, Mommy let me choose a toy in the little toy store. I knew I wanted the green and orange net. I sent away for the . . . "

"Chrysalises," Michael volunteered.

"Remember when they came, Daddy? You hung each one inside the netting. There was nothing to do but wait, but for once, I didn't mind. I would come home from school every day and stare at the netting. Waiting for something to happen."

"You were very patient," Michael put in.

"One day, there were butterflies! They were sooooo beautiful. But then . . . "

"It got harder," Michael said softly.

"I couldn't let them go. I knew it was time, but I just couldn't."
Her eyes were filling with tears.

"I crouched down and I could see four butterflies fluttering around the net in circles. They were ready to be free. But I loved them. I loved coming home from school to see them. I took them outside, but I couldn't do it. I couldn't let them go. I ran into the house, and Mommy came and got me. 'It's time,' she said. She seemed so sure. So I went back outside and opened the top of the net and let one of the butterflies go."

She was remembering the day so vividly. I realized again that the moments our children recall most powerfully are rarely the moments *we* remember. We force photos into frames, more concerned with the quality of the image than its import, memorializing moments almost randomly.

"I opened the net again and two flew out together. They flew from branch to branch, never leaving each other's side. I looked down at the fourth butterfly, who still hadn't moved. I was watching her. All of a sudden she started to flutter her wings, faster and faster, until she was out of the net. I closed my eyes, trying not to cry."

Tancredi lifted his red glass, as if about to propose a toast. I could see that his eyes were crimson as well.

"Then I felt something on my arm. It was the tiny butterfly."
Chiara drew a breath.

"'It's okay,' I whispered. 'You can go.' And she did."

"*Then what?*" Chiara was transfixed.

"I walked back inside, holding the empty net."
We were silent. Ruth had tears in her eyes.

"You were a good mommy to those butterflies," I said, after a moment.

I wanted to be a good mommy to her and to Isabel. They

offered so much more than we ever knew to hope for: Isabel's interest in the Peloponnesian War. Charlotte's love of pets.

Let them be who they are.

When the girls went off to play, the men repaired to the living room. "Wow. That was some story," Ruth said into the silence.

"It was a very big moment for her."

"Should you get her more butterflies?"

"No. But she still thinks about them. She still looks for them."

"She's a better mother to those butterflies than my mother was to me."

"Me, too."

"My mother spent days painting rows of dots on the kitchen walls. Obsessively."

My mother. Where would I begin? "We weren't a very good match. I don't think she really liked me."

"She loved you," Michael insisted, from the next room.

"She *loved* me. But we weren't a good fit. I think I made her nervous. I was so introspective and remote. She liked my brothers better. They were easier to love. I'm not sure she likes Isabel either. Isabel's too much like me."

I thought back to my mother's comment that Isabel might be being abused, and shuddered.

"Maybe she was jealous," Ruth ventured.

"Of what? I was so gawky and uncomfortable. And morose."

"I bet you weren't," Ruth said kindly. "I bet you were sparkly, like Charlotte."

"No. I was very inward, like Isabel."

"Yes," Ruth agreed. "But at least she reads."

As we walked home, a crescent moon rested on the sheet of sky, like an eyelash. Michael and Charlotte moved ahead, chatting gaily, energized by the conviviality of the feast. Stars flooded a felted sky, and the moon glowed like the pilot light of a furnace. I stopped, tilting my head back to study them.

Something spiralled up from my memory:

Do you want the moon to play with?
And the stars to run away with?
Don't you cry.

Don't you cry. Maybe that was my mother's greatest gift to me: the lullaby she sang, night after night after night. I won't grieve anymore, for the mother I did not have. She lives in the past, in its pastness. I don't need her. I am somebody's mother now.

The moon, protector of all things female, brightened my path, a kind of benediction. It's not so easy to be somebody's mom. We can bring to the task an almost metereological precision, but storms are inevitable. Even Charlotte had learned that, with her butterflies. Lacey will never know this: the satisfactions of motherhood, of a long marriage, of shared passions for Sondheim and sea salt caramels. "Life is a tragedy with a happy ending," Edith Wharton wrote. Maybe that was my story, too, and it might have been Lacey's. This was the happy ending she had been denied.

Once home, I made my way into Isabel's room, thinking she would be awake, but she was dozing.

"Hi," she said sleepily.

"I didn't mean to wake you. I just wanted to make sure you were breathing. I just wanted to *smell* you."

"Mooommm," she groaned. Then, "Can you come in?"

I slid under the covers next to her. I could feel the heat where her body had been. I always loved that her nickname and her state of being were one and the same. So declarative, so unassailable. Isabel *is*.

"I remember when you were born, you slithered up my chest and tucked your head under my chin."

"Yuck."

"No, it was amazing. And Daddy was so nervous. He kept asking, 'Is she supposed to be so *blue*?'"

"Was I blue?"

"Yes, briefly. They took you away, to bathe you, and I tried to memorize every freckle, to make sure they gave the same baby back."

"Do you think they did?"

"I do. But it doesn't matter. I like this one." I kissed her on the top of the head. "I'm going to keep her."

For as long as I can. Already I could feel time slipping away, not the whiplash of trauma, but the steady, necessary creep of change. On how many more occasions will I be invited under the sheets?

I was silent for a moment. "What's the worst thing I ever did?"

I expected her to hesitate before responding—or at least, to *seem* to hesitate—but her grievances were more easily accessed than a new app. "Once I ran into your room in the middle of the night because there were all these lights in the street, and I thought they were ghosts. Driving."

"And?"

"And you told me ghosts didn't need cars because they *fly*."

"Was that bad?"

"Yes! There *are* no ghosts. That's what you should have told me!"

I could see now that all she'd wanted was for me to say, "You're safe." I didn't know that, because I never was.

"Is is too late?" I asked.

"For what?"

"To apologize?"

"No. It's never too late."

"I'm so sorry, sweetie." I kissed her forehead. "I really am. I'm so sorry that I was absent or distant . . . "

But she was falling asleep. She turned to one side, as if to vacate the pillow for me, out of her deepest generosity. I marveled that she could generate such heat. She can do *anything,* if she can produce the warmth, the consolation, of this pillow.

She can do anything.

And I know she will.

In the next room, Michael was performing Charlotte's elaborate nighttime rituals, which included kissing Sammy, the stuffed sea lion, good night. Sammy accompanied us on all our trips, including to England, where she was accidently caught up in a hotel sheet and plunged down the laundry chute. Michael searched for her everywhere, while I comforted Charlotte, who was nearly inconsolable.

Then a bellman knocked on the door. "We have a fox here. Is it yours?"

Charlotte was grateful, but also slightly indignant: "It's not a fox! How many foxes have *flippers*?"

Let them be who they are.

Now, in Charlotte's room, Sammy had been pacified. "Love you," Charlotte said.

I heard Michael reply: "I love you, too."

"Good night, Isabel. I love you!" Charlotte trilled, ever hopeful for a response.

"Good night. I love you, too."

"Will you say good night to Sammy?"

Isabel didn't even hesitate. "No."

They would have to figure out this sister thing together.

Let them be who they are.

Emma the dog drew near, as the darkness settled around us. There was a profound sense of rightness. Nothing was amiss. We were linked as a family: balanced by Michael's buoyancy; Isabel's sensitivity; Charlotte's empathy; by the fox with flippers, also so recently, miraculously redeemed. This is all there is—this is *ecstasy*—the direct, the known, the knowable. The "clucking domesticities." (Although Charlotte's guinea pigs do not cluck, they purr.) Everything I wanted was here, and it always had been. Finally I could see that.

I could yield to the claims of peace, to the succor of sleep.

56.

A week later, driving with my daughters, I stopped at the corner of Entrada and the Pacific Coast Highway. This traffic light was notoriously lengthy, and I routinely fell into an aboriginal dream state while waiting for it to change. But the chatter of my daughters rose up from the backseat.

"Mrs. Haskell has chickens," Charlotte announced.

"Who's Mrs. Haskell?"

"My *teacher*."

"Oh, *that* Mrs. Haskell."

"She has chickens."

"That's lovely." I was only half paying attention, trying to navigate this turn.

"It's not lovely," Isabel countered. "Having chickens on a *farm* is lovely. When you live in an apartment? That's just eccentric."

I laughed. "I guess you're right."

There was a man sweeping the street, whom I often saw at this corner. In his walk, part shuffle, part swagger, he reminded me of Joe. Only in L.A. would the man on the street corner have a kind of movie star charisma. I'll have to tell my daughters about Joe one day. But there will be time.

Beyond the man was a sign: CAUTION: ENTERING TSUNAMI HAZARD ZONE.

I laughed. *When did the quiet little beach near our house become a tsunami hazard zone?* I made a note to tell Michael, so he could photograph our daughters next to the sign for our collection of portraits: all those hasty shots near hazardous waste sites and the mating grounds of wild boars.

I thought about this beach, how close I had come to losing Isabel, to never having Charlotte, to betraying Michael in ways that could not be repaired. I had missed the point of the *Tashlich* ceremony, but now I understood why the Hebrew word for "water" begins and ends with the same letter, though the letter is written differently at the beginning and end of the word. That's how much water—the idea of it, the *experience* of it—can transform you.

Suddenly I pulled over.

"Let's get out," I cried, tugging off my shoes.

"Mommy, *what are you doing?*" Charlotte was shocked.

"Let's put our feet in the water."

"But you don't like to get wet!"

"I need to get used to it. Remember, like you did? You wouldn't let us wash your face for ages."

"A lot of my freckles were dirt!"

"I love the water," Isabel murmured, mermaid hair billowing behind.

The girls and I gambolled over the dune, our feet sinking heavily into the sand. Charlotte found a stalk of seaweed, raucously popping its pods. Isabel carefully aligned her sneakers, perhaps remembering a time when *she* had gone missing. Above us, a caucus of seagulls squalled.

I could see now that some larger force, of grace or redemption, had carried me to California, helped me find Michael. Brought my daughters to me and, in spite of many fissures, kept them close. For it was they who forced me to be *of* the world when they came into it.

I gave them life.

But they taught me to breathe.

WHOOOOSH! Isabel splashed me.

I laughed and splashed her back.

"Why don't you like to get wet?" she asked mischievously. "Are you afraid you'll melt?"

"What makes me melt—in a good way—are the moments we're all together."

She smiled and reached for my hand.

We waded gingerly, gratefully, into the water, sea creatures burrowing beneath our feet. There was the predictable detritus: a Styrofoam cup, a ribbon of plastic, a cigarette stub. But the water also teemed with unimaginable riches: whelks and mollusks and sea urchins; garibaldis and cardinal fish, floating freely in their gorgeous hues.

"Wait!" Charlotte shrieked, galloping toward us over the sand.

She cast away the seaweed and grabbed my other hand.

I wanted to tell her to roll up her pants, but I didn't. Sand, like the fairy sparkle coating every surface in my house, is the happy wage of having children. It is proof of the alchemy of grace.

I had been the beneficiary of so much grace, although it had taken me a long time to see it. Maybe that's what the time was for. For time, too, is a dance, stringing together, like a collar of pearls, all we have been and all we will be. All we are *meant* to be, if we can turn our loss, our grief, to grace. If we can accept the moments that are here, *right here,* tangible and fully imagined, as opportunities for liberation, for joy. Moments that bind and release us, that renew us, that define us, that redeem us, that will remain long after the sky has darkened and the sand has cooled.

I want to fill these moments with all I can offer: to be strong hopeful playful balanced brave.

"Onward!" I cried, and the girls laughed, and a sea bird called, the horizon beckoning, as we surged forward into the water, into the deep.

ACKNOWLEDGMENTS

My husband urged me to write this memoir, never suspecting it would become a love letter: to him, our children, and the life we share. He critiqued more drafts than can be counted, embracing the book in all its iterations. He never balked at its most vexing (which is to say, most personal) themes. Ever the lawyer, Michael offered recollections as specific as depositions, but with infinitely more color, humor and detail. Above all, he brought a generosity of spirit—an acceptance— that became the book's anthem. He saw me, heard me, *read* me, and loved me still.

I'm grateful, too, for all the friends who offered notes, snacks and ongoing encouragement, including Pamela S. Bohn, Brandel France de Bravo, Nancy Dodge, Anna Dylan, David Hirson, Phyllis Moberly, Cole Moss, Elisa Petrini, Susan Jacoby Stern and Joel Stern, and Jack Viertel. Several people were especially generous with their time, including Susan Gates, Mikki del Monico, Mary Tanner, and Janet M. Wolfe. I hope my book reflects the sensitive readings they lavished on it.

Darby Bayliss, Cindy Bitterman, Victoria Godfrey, and Deirdre Higgins remained dear friends long after our book group gave up actually reading books. Our periodic meetings stand out like a string of lights during some dark, difficult times. Writing this book taught me about the balm of friendship and the many consolations of connection. All these people were my mentors in this regard.

But it was my book agent, Jeff Kleinman, who found a way to tell my story, and his insights helped bring the many narrative threads to heel. His honesty and powers of persuasion are truly formidable. If my book is, in essence, about learning to ask for help, Jeff rewarded that request every time we spoke.

I was equally fortunate in my editor at Seal Press, Laura Mazer, whose warmth is as winning as her intelligence. From our first conversation, it was clear that she knew how—in her words—to make my story "sing." She had an intuitive understanding of my book, and of the fears and doubts that occasionally threatened to derail it. My gratitude to her goes beyond words.

I owe thanks, too, to everyone who guided my book into the world with kindness and diligence: Donna Galassi, Seal's Vice President and Associate Publisher, and Associate Publicist Molly Conway; Emi Battaglia and Laura Rossi Totten, who brought energy and ideas to the project at a crucial moment; and Nancy Hancock, who proved endlessly creative in helping me navigate the world, online and off.

Thanks also to Julie Pinkerton, whose copyedit was as thoughtful as it was thorough, and Rosemary Ahern, who brought her prodigious editorial skills to several drafts. Laura Klynstra's gorgeous cover kept me company during many months of writing, and Tabitha Lahr's design gave the book an airy elegance.

I am greatly indebted to Jonathan Brecher, Brian Fortman, and Marc Golden for tackling the legal and logistical issues that always gave me a headache, and to Keith Parker and Terence Roberts for technical support and welcome admonitions to "keep the faith." My heartfelt thanks go to Aida Jaco-Cortes and Benita Perez, for kindnesses too numerous to mention, and Rebecca Witjas, for urging me to dance again.

I also want to acknowledge several writers whose work helped me chart my course: Tad Friend for his article on Golden Gate suicides in *The New Yorker*; Jennifer Senior for her exploration of loneliness in *New York* magazine, and Diane Ackerman for her thoughts on the transforming power of love in *The New York Times*.

But my greatest debt is to the family and friends of the woman who became Lacey. I thank them for talking to me, for trusting me. Their candor was another unexpected benefaction. I hope I have honored that gift in the portrait that emerged.

Finally, I want to thank my daughters, Isabel and Charlotte, with apologies for all the late nights holed up in my attic office. They believed in my book and allowed me the space and freedom to write it, never knowing exactly what it was I was working on, or why it mattered to me. They are my life, my world, and all my words are for them. They have brightened every moment, and made every pleasure real.

Los Angeles
2016

ABOUT THE AUTHOR

Jessica Teich graduated *summa cum laude* from Yale and received an M.Phil degree from Oxford, where she was a Rhodes scholar. Her previous book, *Trees Make The Best Mobiles: Simple Ways To Raise Your Child In A Complex World,* appeared in *Vanity Fair, People, Us,* and *The Chicago Tribune,* and was featured on the *Today* show. For almost a decade, Teich worked as a literary manager at the Mark Taper Forum, commissioning and developing plays. She subsequently received a grant to write and direct a movie for the Directing Workshop for Women at the American Film Institute. Teich served as head of the Biography committee for the *Los Angeles Times* Book Prize, and her articles have appeared in *The Washington Post,* the *Los Angeles Times,* and numerous other publications. She lives in Los Angeles with her husband, two daughters, and dog.

SELECTED TITLES FROM SEAL PRESS

Shades of Blue: Writers on Depression, Suicide, and Feeling Blue, edited by Amy Ferris. $16.00, 978-1-58005-595-6. This anthology collects stories from well-known writers about depression, sadness, and attempted suicide, offering empathy to those who have been affected by these issues.

Yogalosophy for Inner Strength: 12 Weeks to Heal Your Heart and Embrace Joy, by Mandy Ingber, $24, 978-1-58005-593-2. Building on the concepts in her *New York Times* best-selling book *Yogalosophy,* Mandy Ingber, fitness and wellness instructor to the stars, now gives us a revolutionary and inspiring self-care program to uplift and strengthen the alignment of mind, body, heart, and spirit during times of adversity like loss, transition, grief, or heartbreak.

Riding Fury Home: A Memoir, by Chana Wilson. $17.00, 978-1-58005-432-4. A shattering, exquisitely written account of one family's struggle against homophobia and mental illness in a changing world—and a powerful story of healing, forgiveness, and redemption.

All the Things We Never Knew: Chasing the Chaos of Mental Illness, by Sheila Hamilton. $24.00, 978-1-58005-584-0. A reporter chases the biggest story of her life—her husband's descent into mental illness.

How Does That Make You Feel: True Confessions from Both Sides of the Therapy Couch, edited by Sherry Amatenstein. $16, 978-1-58005- 624-3. *How Does That Make You Feel?* obliterates the boundaries between the shrink and the one being shrunk with unabashedly candid writers breaking confidentiality and telling all about their experiences in therapy.

Invisible Girls: The Truth about Sexual Abuse, by Dr. Patti Feuereisen with Caroline Pincus. $16.95, 978-1-58005-301-3. An important book for teenage girls, young women, and those who care about them, *Invisible Girls* provides hope and encouragement to sexual abuse survivors by showing that they're not alone and that there are many roads to healing.

Find Seal Press Online
sealpress.com
@sealpress
Facebook | Twitter | Instagram | Tumblr | Pinterest